UNSTOPPABLE

BEYOND LIMITS

REAL STORIES. REAL STRUGGLES. REAL SUCCESS

JOHNATHAN MILLER

REAL STORIES. REAL STRUGGLES. REAL SUCCESS

UNSTOPPABLE

**BIG CHANGES
REMARKABLE RESULTS**

BEYOND LIMITS

FROM STRUGGLES TO
SUCCESS IN THE MODERN
AMERICAN DREAM

REIMAGINED-THE AMERICAN DREAM

Why is it that some people can rise from nothing to achieve extraordinary success, while others struggle just to stay afloat? Is it luck? Timing? Or is it something deeper—something within us all that, when unlocked, can turn even the darkest moments into the brightest triumphs?

You see, we all grew up hearing about the American Dream. The promise that if you work hard enough, you can achieve anything. But let's be real for a second—the world has changed, and for a lot of folks, that dream feels more like a fantasy. Stagnant wages, mounting debt, and a job market that seems to favor automation over people can make the idea of "making it" seem impossible.

Maybe you're feeling that right now. Maybe you've lost a job, faced rejection, or watched your savings dwindle as bills pile up. You're not alone. Millions of Americans are feeling the same frustration, the same fear, the same hopelessness.

But here's the thing—hitting rock bottom doesn't mean you're done. In fact, it can be the very thing that propels you to heights you never imagined. This book is about that moment when everything seems lost, but something inside you refuses to give up. It's about the grit, the determination, and the sheer willpower to turn it all around.

UNSTOPPABLE

Let me introduce you to people who have been where you are—people who were down and out, at the end of their rope, but who found a way to flip the script. These are not just tales of financial success; these are stories of real struggle, pain, and frustration. But they're also stories of incredible resilience, creativity, and the relentless pursuit of a better life.

Take Sarah, for example. She was a single mom, working three jobs just to keep the lights on. She was drowning in debt and felt like she was failing her kids. But one day, after yet another sleepless night, something clicked. She realized she can't keep living like this. Sarah didn't have a fancy degree or a big network, but she had an idea—a simple one—that would turn her life around. Today, she's a millionaire, living proof that it's never too late to rewrite your story.

Or meet Tom, who had built a business from scratch only to watch it crumble during an economic downturn. He lost everything—his savings, his home, his confidence. But instead of giving up, Tom dug deep, found a new passion, and turned it into a multimillion-dollar venture. His story isn't just about bouncing back; it's about reinventing yourself in the face of overwhelming odds.

These stories aren't fairy tales. They're real. They're raw. And they're a reminder that no matter how tough things get, there's always a way out. You just have to find it.

In this book, you'll discover the mindset shifts, the small steps, and the brilliant ideas that transformed ordinary lives into extraordinary ones. You'll learn how to turn your own setbacks into stepping stones, and how to create a blueprint for success that works for you —whether you're starting from scratch or trying to rebuild.

So, if you're ready to stop dreaming and start doing, if you're ready to take control of your future and build something incredible out of the ashes, then keep reading. The journey from rock bottom to riches isn't easy, but it's possible. And it starts right here, right now.

Let's get to work.

HITTING ROCK BOTTOM

THE CATALYST FOR CHANGE

Imagine waking up one day and realizing that everything you've worked for is gone. The job you thought was secure? Gone. The savings you painstakingly built? Wiped out. The plans you had for your future? Suddenly feel like a cruel joke. It's that gut-wrenching moment when you're staring at your bills, your empty bank account, and the pile of rejection letters, wondering how the hell you got here.

That's exactly where Mike found himself. Just a few years ago, Mike had it all—a good job, a comfortable home, and a sense of security that he thought was unshakeable. But then, the unthinkable happened. The company he'd dedicated his life to for over a decade went under, and just like that, he was out of a job. No severance, no warning, just a "sorry, we're closing up shop."

At first, Mike thought he could bounce back. He updated his resume, applied to every job he could find, even the ones he was way overqualified for. But as the weeks turned into months, the rejection emails piled up. His savings dwindled, and with every bill that went unpaid, the anxiety tightened its grip on him. The mortgage payments started slipping, credit card debts mounted, and before long, Mike was facing foreclosure on his home.

UNSTOPPABLE

Mike wasn't just broke; he was broken. He felt like a failure—a man who couldn't provide for his family, who had lost everything he'd worked so hard to build. He stopped answering phone calls from friends, too ashamed to admit what was happening. He was drowning in shame, anger, and frustration, questioning everything he'd ever believed about hard work and the so-called American Dream.

One cold December night, after a particularly brutal day of job hunting and coming up empty, Mike sat in his darkened living room, staring at the eviction notice on his coffee table. He was exhausted, both physically and mentally. He'd hit rock bottom, and it felt like there was no way out.

But here's the thing about rock bottom—it's a solid foundation. It's the place where you can either give up or dig deep and start climbing. And that night, Mike made a choice. He could either let his circumstances define him, or he could redefine himself. He realized that no one was coming to save him, and that if he wanted to change his life, he'd have to do it himself.

So, he did something he'd never considered before. He took a risk. With nothing left to lose, Mike decided to start a small side business, something he could do from his garage with the little bit of money he had left. It wasn't glamorous—it was a humble lawn care service. But Mike threw himself into it with everything he had, driven by the determination to rebuild his life from the ground up.

UNSTOPPABLE

At first, it was slow going. He handed out flyers, knocked on doors, and worked long hours for little pay. But as the weeks passed, word spread. Mike's attention to detail and relentless work ethic began to attract more clients. The business grew, and with it, Mike's confidence. He started hiring a few employees, investing in better equipment, and expanding his services.

Fast forward a couple of years, and that little lawn care business? It's now a thriving landscaping company, generating over a million dollars a year. Mike isn't just back on his feet; he's stronger than ever. He's paid off his debts, bought a new home, and even started putting money away for his kids' college funds.

But more than the financial success, Mike learned something invaluable—something money can't buy. He learned that when you're pushed to your absolute limit, that's when you find out what you're really made of. And that sometimes, the path to success isn't the one you planned, but the one you forge when you refuse to quit.

Mike's story isn't unique. Across America, there are countless people who have found themselves in that same dark place, facing impossible odds. But it's in those moments of despair that the seeds of greatness are planted. Rock bottom isn't the end; it's the beginning of something new—if you're willing to dig deep, take risks, and fight for your future.

UNSTOPPABLE

In the stories ahead, you'll meet more people like Mike—ordinary Americans who faced extraordinary challenges and came out on top. Their stories are filled with pain, frustration, and moments of doubt, but they're also filled with hope, resilience, and the kind of brilliant ideas that can turn anyone into a millionaire.

So, if you're struggling right now, if you're feeling like the walls are closing in and there's no way out, remember this: Rock bottom isn't your final destination. It's the launching pad for your comeback. Keep reading, because the stories that follow just might be the spark you need to start your own journey from rags to riches.

Let's dive in.

UNSTOPPABLE

THE MINDSET SHIFT

2

FROM SCARCITY TO ABUNDANCE

When you're stuck in a cycle of struggle, it can feel like the whole world is against you. Bills are piling up, your bank account is barely hanging on, and every time you think you're about to catch a break, life seems to hit you with another setback. It's easy to start believing that this is just how things are meant to be—like the universe has decided that you're destined to scrape by while others thrive.

That's exactly how Jessica felt. She'd always been a hard worker, juggling multiple jobs while raising two kids on her own. But no matter how hard she worked, it never seemed to be enough. Her paycheck would be gone before the end of the month, eaten up by rent, utilities, and the never-ending stream of unexpected expenses. The stress was constant, gnawing at her day and night. She was living in survival mode, and it was exhausting.

Jessica wasn't just broke; she was broken. She'd started to believe that maybe she wasn't cut out for anything better. Maybe this was just her lot in life—to work herself to the bone and have nothing to show for it. Every time she saw someone else succeed, she felt a pang of jealousy and a heavy sense of resignation. Why did it seem so easy for others? What did they have that she didn't?

UNSTOPPABLE

One night, after a particularly grueling double shift, Jessica collapsed onto her couch, too tired to even think straight. But as she sat there in the quiet, something inside her snapped. She was sick and tired of feeling sick and tired. She was done with being a victim of her circumstances. Jessica realized that if she wanted to change her life, she had to start with changing the way she thought about herself and her situation.

She didn't know it then, but that moment was the beginning of a complete transformation. Jessica decided to stop focusing on what she didn't have and started focusing on what she could do. She began to see her struggles not as a curse, but as a challenge—a puzzle she could solve if she approached it the right way.

Jessica dove into self-help books and podcasts, soaking up everything she could about mindset, abundance, and success. She started small, with daily affirmations, telling herself that she deserved success, that she was capable of achieving more. At first, it felt awkward, like she was lying to herself. But slowly, those words began to take root. She started to believe them.

The biggest shift came when she stumbled across a book on the power of mindset—a book that talked about how your thoughts shape your reality. It was like a lightbulb went off. Jessica realized that she had been living with a scarcity mindset, always afraid that there wasn't enough—enough money, enough opportunities, enough luck—to go around. And because she believed it, that's exactly what she got.

But what if she could change that? What if, instead of seeing the world as full of limits, she started seeing it as full of possibilities?

Jessica decided to put it to the test. She started looking for opportunities, even in the most unlikely places. She noticed that her neighbor was struggling to keep up with her yard work, so Jessica offered to help—at a price, of course. Word spread, and soon she had a handful of clients who were happy to pay her for yard work, house cleaning, and other odd jobs.

It wasn't glamorous, and it certainly wasn't a get-rich-quick scheme. But it was a start. And more importantly, it was a shift. Jessica wasn't just working to survive anymore; she was working with a purpose. She was building something.

As she continued to work on her mindset, Jessica's life began to change in ways she never expected. Opportunities seemed to appear out of nowhere—like the time she overheard a conversation at the grocery store about a local business that was looking for someone to manage their social media. Jessica had never done that kind of work before, but she'd been teaching herself the basics online. She took a deep breath, introduced herself, and walked away with a new client.

Jessica's side gigs grew into a small business, and her small business grew into something bigger than she'd ever imagined. Within two years, she was making more money than she ever had in her life—not by working harder, but by working smarter. She had shifted her mindset from scarcity to abundance, and the results were nothing short of miraculous.

Today, Jessica isn't just financially secure; she's thriving. She's paid off her debt, bought a home for her family, and even started a savings account for her kids' college fund. But more than the money, it's the mindset shift that has changed her life. Jessica knows now that abundance isn't just about money—it's about possibilities, opportunities, and believing that you deserve them.

Her story is a powerful reminder that the first step to changing your life isn't about getting a better job or making more money. It's about changing the way you think. If you believe that you're stuck, that there's never enough, then that's exactly what you'll experience. But if you can shift your mindset—if you can start seeing the world as full of opportunities—then anything is possible.

In the next chapter, we'll dive into the power of persistence. You'll meet someone who faced failure after failure, but never gave up. Their story will show you that sometimes, the road to success is paved with setbacks, but if you keep moving forward, you'll eventually get where you're meant to be.

So, if you're ready to shift your mindset and start seeing the world through a lens of abundance, keep reading. The stories that follow will show you just how powerful a change in perspective can be, and how it might just be the key to unlocking the life you've always dreamed of.

THE POWER OF PERSISTENCE

TURNING SETBACKS INTO STEPPING STONES

Failure. It's a word that strikes fear into the hearts of most people. We're taught from a young age that failing is something to be ashamed of, something to avoid at all costs. But what if failure isn't the end? What if it's just the beginning of something bigger—something better than you ever imagined?

Meet David. David was always the kind of guy who took pride in his work. He started his own business in his early twenties, full of hope and ambition, believing that hard work and determination would be enough to guarantee success. And for a while, it seemed like he was right. His business—a small but growing tech startup—was doing well. He had clients, he had momentum, and he had a plan.

But then, out of nowhere, things started to fall apart. One of his biggest clients suddenly pulled out, citing budget cuts. Then another followed suit. David's business, which had been thriving just months earlier, was suddenly on life support. He tried everything he could think of to save it—cutting costs, taking on more work himself, even dipping into his personal savings to keep the lights on. But it wasn't enough.

UNSTOPPABLE

Within a year, David was forced to shut down the business he had poured his heart and soul into. He was devastated. It felt like everything he'd worked for had been for nothing. He had failed, and the weight of that failure was crushing. He withdrew from friends and family, embarrassed to admit that he'd lost it all. The shame and frustration ate at him every day.

But as the weeks turned into months, something began to shift in David. He realized that while he had lost his business, he hadn't lost his skills, his knowledge, or his passion. The fire inside him hadn't gone out; it had just dimmed a little. And he knew that if he wanted to reclaim his life, he couldn't let this failure define him.

David started to see his failure not as a dead end, but as a detour—an opportunity to learn and grow. He began to study the mistakes he had made, analyzing every decision, every misstep, trying to understand where things had gone wrong. He didn't shy away from the pain of those memories; instead, he faced them head-on, determined to turn them into lessons he could use in the future.

And then, he did something that most people would never dream of doing: he started over. With nothing but a few thousand dollars and a head full of hard-earned lessons, David launched a new business. This time, he was smarter, more cautious, and more determined than ever before. He used the pain of his past failure as fuel, pushing him to work harder, think more strategically, and never take anything for granted.

UNSTOPPABLE

At first, it was slow going. David struggled to regain the confidence of clients who had seen his previous business go under. He faced countless rejections, late nights, and moments of doubt. But he kept going, one step at a time, believing that persistence would eventually pay off.

And it did.

David's new business began to pick up steam. The lessons he had learned from his failure helped him avoid the pitfalls that had tripped him up before. He was more resilient, more adaptable, and more willing to take calculated risks. Within a few years, his new venture was thriving, far surpassing the success of his first business.

But the real victory wasn't just in the money he made or the clients he landed. It was in the knowledge that he had turned his greatest failure into his greatest asset. David realized that failure wasn't something to be feared—it was something to be embraced. Because every time you fail, you're one step closer to figuring out what works.

David's story is a testament to the power of persistence. It's proof that setbacks don't have to be the end of your journey. In fact, they can be the very thing that propels you forward, if you're willing to learn from them and keep pushing ahead.

You see, success isn't about never failing; it's about how you handle failure when it inevitably comes. It's about getting back up after you've been knocked down, dusting yourself off, and trying again. It's about persistence—the kind of dogged determination that refuses to quit, even when the odds are stacked against you.

So, if you're in the middle of a setback right now, if you feel like you've hit a wall and there's no way through, remember this: Every successful person you admire has faced failure at some point. They've been where you are, feeling the same frustration, the same hopelessness. But what sets them apart is that they didn't let it stop them. They kept going. And you can, too.

In the next chapter, we'll explore the importance of finding your niche—how honing in on what makes you unique can be the key to unlocking success. You'll meet someone who turned their passion into a multimillion-dollar business by tapping into a market that most people didn't even know existed. It's a story that will inspire you to think differently about what's possible for your own life.

So, keep reading. The journey isn't over yet, and the best is still to come. Let's turn those setbacks into stepping stones, and keep moving forward, one step closer to the success you've always dreamed of.

FINDING YOUR NICHE

THE PATH TO UNCOMMON SUCCESS

Sometimes, the key to success isn't about being the best at something—it's about being different. It's about finding that one thing that sets you apart, that one passion or skill that, when tapped into, can open doors you never knew existed. But discovering your niche isn't always straightforward. Often, it takes a journey through frustration, doubt, and plenty of false starts before you stumble upon the thing that makes you truly unique.

That's exactly what happened to Lisa. Lisa was like so many of us—she went to college, got a degree, and landed a decent job in marketing. It paid the bills, but it didn't light her up. Every day felt the same, a monotonous grind that left her feeling unfulfilled. She knew she was capable of more, but she didn't know what that "more" was.

She tried everything she could think of to shake off that feeling of emptiness. She took on new projects at work, hoping they'd reignite her passion. She dabbled in side hustles, from freelance writing to selling homemade crafts online. But nothing stuck. Each venture felt like just another dead end, leaving her more frustrated and lost than before.

UNSTOPPABLE

As the years passed, Lisa felt like she was running out of time. She was in her thirties, watching friends settle into careers they loved, while she was stuck in a job that drained her soul. The pressure to find her calling was becoming unbearable, and the more she searched, the more elusive it seemed. She started to wonder if she'd ever find something she was truly passionate about—something that could become more than just a paycheck.

Then, one rainy afternoon, something unexpected happened. Lisa had always loved baking, a hobby she picked up from her grandmother. But it was just that—a hobby. She never thought much about it, other than how it brought her a sense of peace after a long day. But on this particular day, as she was scrolling through social media, she came across a post about someone who had turned their love for baking into a successful online business.

The idea hit her like a bolt of lightning. What if she could do the same? What if the thing she'd been searching for was right in front of her all along?

At first, the idea felt ridiculous. Who would want to buy her baked goods when there were so many professional bakeries out there? But the more she thought about it, the more the idea took hold. Lisa realized that her love for baking wasn't just about making cookies and cakes—it was about the joy it brought to others, the way it connected her to her grandmother's memory, and the creativity it allowed her to express.

UNSTOPPABLE

But she knew she needed a unique angle—something that would set her apart in a crowded market. So, she started experimenting. She combined her passion for baking with another love—health and wellness. Lisa began creating healthier versions of classic desserts, using all-natural, organic ingredients, and tweaking recipes to make them gluten-free, dairy-free, or low in sugar. She wanted to prove that healthy desserts could still taste incredible.

At first, it was just an experiment, something she did for fun in her free time. But when she started sharing her creations with friends and coworkers, the response was overwhelming. People loved her desserts—they couldn't believe they were healthy. They started asking if she sold them, if she could make them for parties or special occasions.

That's when Lisa realized she was onto something. She wasn't just another baker; she had found her niche. She was filling a gap in the market that no one else was addressing—delicious, healthy desserts that didn't compromise on flavor.

Lisa took the leap. She quit her job, rented a small commercial kitchen, and launched her own brand—"Guilt-Free Goodies." She started small, selling at local farmers' markets and through a simple website she set up herself. The early days were tough. There were sleepless nights, moments of doubt, and plenty of mistakes. But every time she saw a customer's face light up after tasting one of her creations, she knew she was on the right path.

Word spread quickly. People loved her desserts, not just because they were healthy, but because they were genuinely delicious. She began landing contracts with local health food stores, then with larger retailers. Within a few years, Guilt-Free Goodies had become a thriving business, with products sold nationwide and a loyal customer base that couldn't get enough of her unique treats.

Lisa's journey wasn't easy, and it wasn't straightforward. It took years of frustration and false starts before she found her niche. But once she did, everything clicked into place. Her passion, combined with her unique angle, was the recipe for success.

What Lisa's story teaches us is that finding your niche isn't always about discovering something new—it's about looking at what you already love and finding a way to make it your own. It's about blending your passions, your skills, and your experiences into something that's uniquely you. And when you do, you don't just stand out—you shine.

So, if you're feeling stuck, if you're wondering if you'll ever find your place in the world, take a step back. Look at what you love, what you're good at, and how you can bring something new to the table. Your niche might be closer than you think.

UNSTOPPABLE

In the next chapter, we'll explore how one simple idea can be the spark that changes everything. You'll meet someone who turned a small, seemingly insignificant thought into a multimillion-dollar business. It's a story that will inspire you to start thinking bigger and to see the potential in even the smallest ideas.

Keep reading, because the next **big** idea could be yours. Let's find it together.

THE MILLION-DOLLAR IDEA

CREATIVITY MEETS OPPORTUNITY

Sometimes, success doesn't come from a grand plan or a perfect strategy. Sometimes, it starts with just a spark—a simple idea that grows into something far bigger than you ever imagined. But here's the catch: recognizing that spark, and having the guts to chase it, even when it seems like nothing more than a flicker.

This is exactly how it happened for Alex. Alex was the kind of guy who always had a side hustle. He worked a regular 9-to-5 job in a cubicle, but he never stopped dreaming about something more. He dabbled in everything—selling vintage records on eBay, flipping furniture he found on the curb, even trying his hand at photography. But nothing seemed to take off. Every time one of his ideas fizzled out, he'd shrug it off and tell himself, "Maybe the next one."

But as the years went by, "maybe the next one" started to sound more like a broken record. He was getting older, his friends were settling into steady careers, and he was still stuck, feeling like he was spinning his wheels. He loved his side projects, but they weren't paying the bills. And no matter how hard he tried, he couldn't seem to turn his passion into something real, something sustainable.

UNSTOPPABLE

One night, after a long day at work, Alex was sitting on his couch, scrolling through social media, when he saw something that caught his eye. It was a short video of someone using a phone holder that clipped onto a desk. The video wasn't flashy or high-tech; it was just a simple demonstration. But something about it struck Alex. The holder looked useful—really useful.

Alex had seen plenty of gadgets come and go, but this one was different. It wasn't some gimmick; it was practical, something people might actually need. And in that moment, he had an idea. What if he could create something like that, but better? What if he could design a phone holder that was more versatile, more durable, something that would appeal to people working from home, students, or even travelers?

The idea kept him up that night. He started sketching out designs, thinking about materials, figuring out how he could make it affordable but high-quality. The more he thought about it, the more he realized that this could be the idea he'd been waiting for—the one that could actually work.

But Alex didn't just dream about it. He took action. He researched manufacturers, reached out to suppliers, and started working on prototypes. He spent his evenings and weekends testing different designs, tweaking them until they were just right. It wasn't easy. There were setbacks, like when his first batch of prototypes came back completely wrong, or when he realized he'd underestimated the cost of shipping by a mile. But he didn't give up.

UNSTOPPABLE

Finally, after months of work, he had a product he was proud of. He launched a simple website, set up a few social media accounts, and waited. At first, nothing happened. Days went by with barely any sales. He started to doubt himself, wondering if he'd wasted his time on yet another dead-end idea.

But then, something unexpected happened. A popular tech blog featured his phone holder in a roundup of "must-have" gadgets for remote workers. Overnight, his website was flooded with orders. What started as a trickle turned into a torrent. He could barely keep up with demand. The phone holder was a hit, not just because it was useful, but because it filled a need people didn't even know they had.

Within a year, Alex's side hustle had become a full-fledged business. He expanded his product line, hired a small team, and even started selling on major online platforms. His simple idea—the one he almost dismissed as just another passing thought—had turned into a million-dollar business.

Alex's story isn't just about luck or being in the right place at the right time. It's about seeing an opportunity in something small, something almost ordinary, and having the creativity and determination to turn it into something extraordinary. It's about believing that even the simplest idea can be the spark that changes everything.

UNSTOPPABLE

What Alex learned—and what his story teaches us—is that you don't have to have the next big thing figured out from the start. You just have to start with something. Something that solves a problem, fills a need, or makes life a little easier for someone. And then, you have to chase it down with everything you've got.

So, if you're sitting on an idea right now—no matter how small or insignificant it might seem—don't ignore it. Don't let it pass by because you think it's not big enough or good enough. That idea could be your million-dollar spark, the thing that sets you on a path to success you never imagined.

In the next chapter, we'll talk about how to build a brand that resonates with people—how to take that idea and turn it into something people recognize, trust, and can't wait to tell their friends about. You'll meet someone who took a personal passion and built it into a brand that's now a household name. It's a story that will inspire you to think bigger about what your idea could become.

Keep reading, because the journey from idea to impact is just getting started. Let's find your spark and turn it into a fire.

BUILDING A BRAND

FROM PASSION TO HOUSEHOLD NAME

You've got the idea. Maybe it's a product, a service, or a creative project. It's something you believe in, something you've poured your heart into. But here's the thing—having a great idea is only the beginning. To turn it into something truly successful, you need to build a brand around it. A brand that people connect with, trust, and can't wait to tell others about.

But how do you go from being just another name in a crowded market to becoming the name that everyone knows? How do you take your passion and turn it into a brand that's not just successful, but iconic?

That's where Haley's story comes in.

Haley had always been passionate about fitness. From a young age, she loved working out, learning about nutrition, and helping her friends stay motivated. It wasn't just a hobby; it was a lifestyle. But like many of us, Haley didn't think she could turn her passion into a career. She thought it would always just be something she did on the side, while working a "real" job to pay the bills.

UNSTOPPABLE

After college, Haley took a corporate job in marketing. It was stable, it paid well, and it was what everyone expected her to do. But as the years went by, Haley found herself feeling more and more disconnected from her work. She was good at it, but it didn't light her up. She spent her days counting the hours until she could hit the gym, where she felt most alive.

Then one day, after another soul-crushing day at the office, Haley had a moment of clarity. She realized that she couldn't keep living like this—waking up every day to do something she didn't care about, just to pay the bills. She needed to find a way to turn her passion for fitness into something more. But how?

At first, Haley wasn't sure where to start. She thought about becoming a personal trainer, but that didn't feel like the right fit. Then she considered opening a gym, but the costs were too high. It seemed like every idea she had was met with obstacles. But Haley didn't give up. She kept thinking, kept dreaming, kept searching for the answer.

Then, one night, she was scrolling through social media when she noticed something. There were countless fitness brands out there, but they all looked the same. The same sleek, minimalist logos. The same cookie-cutter slogans. The same perfectly toned models showing off their six-packs. It all felt so... impersonal.

And that's when it hit her. What if she could create a brand that was different? A brand that wasn't just about selling products, but about building a community? A brand that felt personal, authentic, and real—something people could actually connect with, something that made them feel seen and supported?

Haley decided to go for it. She quit her job, cashed out her savings, and launched her own fitness brand—"Real Strength." But this wasn't just another fitness brand. Haley wanted to create something that celebrated all kinds of strength, not just the kind you see in magazines. She wanted to build a community where people of all shapes, sizes, and fitness levels felt welcome and empowered.

At first, Haley started small. She designed a few t-shirts and hoodies with motivational sayings, things that reflected her philosophy of strength as something more than just physical. She began posting workout videos on social media, but they weren't your typical fitness videos. Haley focused on the mental and emotional aspects of fitness—the kind of strength it takes to keep going when life gets tough, the resilience to start over after a setback, the courage to love your body no matter what.

The response was immediate. People connected with her message in a way she never expected. They weren't just buying her clothes; they were buying into her vision. They were sharing her posts, tagging their friends, and sending her messages about how her brand was making a difference in their lives.

Within a few months, Real Strength was taking off. Haley expanded her product line, started hosting fitness challenges, and even launched a podcast where she interviewed people about their own journeys to finding strength. Her brand wasn't just about selling products anymore; it was about building a movement.

As her brand grew, Haley stayed true to her vision. She didn't chase trends or try to be something she wasn't. She kept it real, kept it authentic, and that's what made people love her brand. Real Strength wasn't just a business; it was a community, a source of inspiration, a place where people felt like they belonged.

Today, Real Strength is a multimillion-dollar brand with customers all over the world. But more importantly, it's a brand that makes people feel strong, inside and out. Haley's story is proof that when you build a brand that's authentic, that reflects your true passion, people will respond. They'll connect with it, support it, and help it grow.

So, what can you learn from Haley's journey? It's simple: Don't just create a product, create a brand. A brand that tells a story, that stands for something, that makes people feel something. Be authentic. Be real. And most importantly, be passionate. When you build a brand around your passion, people will notice. They'll care. And they'll come back for more.

In the next stories, we'll explore how to leverage technology to scale your brand, taking it from a small business to a big success. You'll hear from someone who used the power of the internet to turn their brand into a global phenomenon, reaching customers they never dreamed possible. It's a story that will show you how to think big, act boldly, and take your brand to the next level.

Keep reading, because your brand is just getting started. Let's make it something unforgettable.

LEVERAGING TECHNOLOGY

SCALING YOUR SUCCESS

You've built something good—maybe even great. But now comes the real challenge: how do you take it to the next level? How do you turn a small, promising business into a full-blown success story that reaches people far beyond your local community? The answer lies in technology. In today's world, it's the difference between staying small and going big.

But before we dive into the tech, let's talk about Sam. Sam's story starts like a lot of ours—with frustration. For years, Sam had been running a small handmade jewelry business out of her garage. It started as a hobby, something she did on weekends and after work, but over time, it grew. Her friends loved her work, then their friends started buying pieces, and before she knew it, she had a steady stream of customers.

But as much as she loved making jewelry, Sam was stuck. She was doing everything herself—designing, crafting, packaging, shipping, managing orders. And while her customers loved her work, her reach was limited. She was selling at local craft fairs and through word of mouth, but her business wasn't growing the way she wanted. She felt like she was hitting a ceiling, and no matter how hard she worked, she couldn't break through.

UNSTOPPABLE

The frustration was overwhelming. Sam knew her jewelry was good—people told her all the time how much they loved it. But how could she take it further? How could she reach more people without losing the personal touch that made her business special? The thought of scaling up was daunting. She didn't have the budget for a fancy marketing campaign, and the idea of running a big operation felt like it would take her away from the very thing she loved—making the jewelry.

But then, something changed. One evening, while browsing the internet, Sam stumbled upon a story about a small business that had blown up online—thanks to social media. The owner had used Instagram to showcase her products, connect with customers, and build a brand that people couldn't get enough of. It was a lightbulb moment for Sam. Maybe she didn't need a big marketing budget or a huge team—maybe she just needed to use the tools that were right in front of her.

Sam decided to give it a shot. She created an Instagram account for her jewelry, not really knowing what to expect. At first, it was just pictures of her pieces, but soon she started sharing more—photos of her workspace, videos of her creating new designs, behind-the-scenes looks at her process. She began telling the story of her business, one post at a time, letting people in on the passion and craftsmanship behind each piece.

And slowly but surely, it started to work. People began to take notice. Her follower count grew, and with it, her sales. Customers who had never heard of her before were suddenly placing orders from across the country, even from other parts of the world. Sam was amazed. The internet had opened up a whole new world of possibilities—one that didn't require her to sacrifice the personal touch she cared so much about.

But she didn't stop there. As her online presence grew, Sam started exploring other ways technology could help her business. She set up an online store, streamlined her order process, and began using email marketing to stay connected with her customers. She even started offering virtual workshops where she taught people how to make their own jewelry, expanding her brand beyond just products to experiences.

The result? Sam's small, local business transformed into a thriving online brand, with customers from all over the world. She was no longer just a local artisan—she was a global entrepreneur. And the best part? She still did it all from her garage, with the same love and care she'd always put into her work.

Sam's story is a powerful reminder of what's possible when you leverage technology. In today's world, the tools to grow your business are more accessible than ever. Whether it's social media, e-commerce platforms, or digital marketing, technology can help you reach people you never thought possible, without losing the authenticity that makes your brand unique.

But here's the thing—technology is just a tool. It's how you use it that makes the difference. Sam didn't just throw up a website and hope for the best. She used technology to tell her story, to connect with people on a personal level, to share her passion in a way that resonated. That's what made her business take off.

So, if you're looking to scale your success, don't be afraid to embrace the digital world. Start small, experiment, and find the platforms that work for you. Whether it's building a following on social media, setting up an online store, or using email to keep your customers engaged, the opportunities are endless. And remember, it's not about using every tool out there—it's about using the right tools in the right way.

In the next chapter, we'll talk about something that's often overlooked in the pursuit of success: giving back. You'll meet someone who, after achieving financial success, discovered that true wealth isn't just about money—it's about making a difference. It's a story that will inspire you to think about success not just in terms of what you gain, but in what you can give.

UNSTOPPABLE

Keep reading, because the journey doesn't end with making millions. It's about finding meaning in what you do, and how you can use your success to impact the world around you. Let's explore how giving back can be the ultimate measure of success.

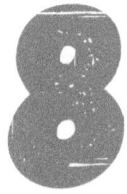  

GIVING BACK

THE ULTIMATE MEASURE OF SUCCESS

You've worked hard. You've fought through setbacks, turned your ideas into reality, and built something you're proud of. Maybe you've even hit that million-dollar mark. But here's the question: Now that you've made it, what's next? What do you do when you've achieved the success you've been chasing?

For a lot of people, the answer is simple: Give back. But that wasn't always the plan for Tyler.

Tyler grew up in a small town, the kind where everyone knows each other's business and opportunities are few and far between. His family didn't have much—his dad worked two jobs, and his mom did everything she could to stretch a dollar. Tyler learned early on that if he wanted something, he'd have to work for it. So, he did. He shoveled snow in the winter, mowed lawns in the summer, and by the time he was a teenager, he was saving up every penny he could.

After high school, Tyler left town for college, determined to make something of himself. He was smart, driven, and more than a little stubborn. He studied business, pulled all-nighters, and by the time he graduated, he'd landed a job at a tech startup. He threw himself into his work, putting in the kind of hours that most people wouldn't even consider. And it paid off. The startup took off, and so did Tyler's career.

UNSTOPPABLE

Within a few years, Tyler was making more money than he'd ever dreamed of. He bought a nice car, a nicer house, and started living the life he'd always wanted. But despite all the success, something didn't feel right. No matter how much money he made, it didn't seem to fill the void he felt inside. He was living the American Dream, but it felt hollow.

It wasn't until one Christmas Eve, when Tyler went back to his hometown to visit his family, that things started to change. He was walking through the old neighborhood when he ran into Mrs. Thompson, his high school English teacher. She was always one of his favorites—tough but fair, and always pushing him to do his best. She asked him how he was doing, and Tyler told her about his success, his job, his life in the city.

Mrs. Thompson smiled, but then she said something that stuck with him. "That's wonderful, Tyler. But what are you doing with it?"

Tyler didn't know what to say. What was he doing with it? He had a big bank account and a fancy job, but what was it all for? That question lingered in his mind for weeks after he left town, gnawing at him, making him question everything he'd been working for.

UNSTOPPABLE

A few months later, Tyler was back in the city, still thinking about that conversation. One day, while sitting in his office, staring at his computer screen, he noticed an email from a local charity. They were looking for donations to help build a community center in a struggling neighbourhood nearby. Without thinking too much about it, Tyler clicked the link and donated a small amount.

But that wasn't the end of it. The charity invited him to visit the neighbourhood, to see the impact his donation would have. Tyler decided to go, thinking it would be a quick visit, a photo op at most. But when he got there, everything changed. He saw the faces of the kids who would benefit from the community center, heard their stories, saw their dreams and hopes despite the challenges they faced.

Something clicked inside Tyler that day. He realized that his success meant nothing if it didn't help others. He had been so focused on climbing the ladder, on making more and more money, that he'd lost sight of what really mattered. He decided right then and there that he was going to do more—give more, help more, be more.

Tyler didn't just write a check and walk away. He got involved. He started volunteering his time, using his business skills to help the charity grow, mentoring young people who needed guidance and support. And the more he gave, the more he felt fulfilled in a way that money had never made him feel.

UNSTOPPABLE

He didn't stop there. Tyler began using his success to support causes he believed in—education, healthcare, housing. He invested in his community, started scholarships for kids from low-income families, and even helped build a program to teach entrepreneurship to underprivileged youth. What started as a simple donation turned into a mission, a purpose that gave his life new meaning.

Tyler's story is a reminder that success isn't just about what you achieve for yourself. It's about what you do with it. The real measure of success isn't the size of your bank account, but the impact you have on the world around you. And sometimes, the greatest rewards come from giving back, from lifting others up and helping them find their own path to success.

So, if you've reached the point where you've achieved your goals, where you've made it to the top, ask yourself the same question Mrs. Thompson asked Tyler: What are you doing with it? How are you using your success to make a difference?

In the final chapter, we'll explore how to sustain that success—how to keep growing, keep giving, and keep finding new ways to make an impact. You'll hear from someone who not only found success but figured out how to maintain it over the long haul. It's a story that will show you that the journey doesn't end when you reach your goal—it's just the beginning of something even greater.

Keep reading, because the best is yet to come. Let's see what's next on your journey to true success.

9

SUSTAINING SUCCESS

THE JOURNEY BEYOND THE FINISH LINE

You've reached the top. The money's rolling in, your business is booming, and you've even found ways to give back. But here's the thing—success isn't a finish line. It's a journey, one that keeps evolving, one that requires constant growth, learning, and adaptation. The real challenge isn't just getting to the top; it's staying there.

That's a lesson Caroline learned the hard way.

Caroline's rise to success was fast and furious. After years of grinding away in a dead-end job, she hit on an idea that changed everything—a subscription box service that delivered healthy, organic snacks right to your door. It was a simple concept, but one that tapped into a growing market of health-conscious consumers who wanted convenience without sacrificing quality.

When Caroline launched her business, she had no idea how quickly it would take off. Within months, she was drowning in orders, barely able to keep up with the demand. It was exciting and overwhelming all at once. She hired more staff, expanded her operations, and started raking in the kind of profits she'd only dreamed of.

UNSTOPPABLE

For a while, everything was perfect. The business was thriving, customers were happy, and Caroline felt like she was on top of the world. But as the months turned into years, cracks started to appear. The market began to change—new competitors entered the space, offering cheaper options or more niche products. Customer tastes evolved, and what was once novel became just another option in an increasingly crowded field.

Caroline, so focused on riding the wave of her initial success, didn't see the warning signs. She kept doing what had worked in the past, assuming that if it had gotten her this far, it would keep working forever. But slowly, her sales began to plateau, then decline. Customers were leaving for newer, flashier brands, and her once-loyal base was shrinking.

It was a punch to the gut. Caroline had poured everything into this business—her time, her energy, her passion—and now it was slipping through her fingers. She felt like she was failing, like all her hard work had been for nothing. The stress of trying to keep the business afloat started to take a toll on her health, her relationships, and her confidence.

One night, after a particularly brutal day of dealing with angry customers and frustrated employees, Caroline sat down and faced the truth: if she didn't make some big changes, her business wasn't going to survive. She realized she'd gotten too comfortable, too complacent. She'd stopped innovating, stopped pushing herself, and the market had passed her by.

But Caroline wasn't ready to give up. She knew that if she wanted to turn things around, she needed to get back to what had made her successful in the first place—her willingness to take risks, to think outside the box, to adapt and evolve. So, she did something she hadn't done in years: she started listening to her customers.

Caroline spent weeks diving into customer feedback, studying market trends, and brainstorming new ideas. She brought in a consultant to help her see things from a different perspective, and she wasn't afraid to make tough decisions—like discontinuing underperforming products or rebranding certain aspects of her business.

One of her biggest moves was to create a new line of subscription boxes that catered to specific dietary needs—gluten-free, keto, vegan—each curated with the same attention to quality that had made her original service so popular. She also ramped up her digital marketing efforts, using social media and influencer partnerships to reach new audiences.

It wasn't easy. The changes took time, and there were plenty of sleepless nights filled with doubt and anxiety. But slowly, things started to turn around. Sales began to climb again, new customers were signing up, and old ones were returning. Caroline's business was no longer just surviving—it was thriving, stronger and more resilient than ever before.

Through it all, Caroline learned that success isn't static. It's dynamic, constantly shifting, and if you're not willing to change with it, you'll get left behind. The journey doesn't end when you hit a milestone; it continues as long as you're willing to keep moving forward, to keep learning, and to keep pushing yourself.

Caroline's story is a powerful reminder that sustaining success requires as much effort—if not more—than achieving it in the first place. It's about staying hungry, staying curious, and never losing sight of the bigger picture. Success is a journey, not a destination, and it's one that requires constant attention and care.

So, if you've made it this far, don't stop. Keep growing, keep innovating, and keep challenging yourself. Success isn't something you achieve once and then hold onto—it's something you have to work at every day.

UNSTOPPABLE

As we wrap up, I want to leave you with this thought: The journey to success is ongoing. There will be highs and lows, victories and setbacks. But if you stay focused, stay resilient, and stay true to yourself, there's no limit to what you can achieve.

The stories you've read in these pages are just the beginning. Your story is still being written, and the next chapter is yours to create. So, go out there, take risks, embrace the challenges, and never stop striving for more. Because the journey doesn't end here—it's just getting started.

Now, it's your turn to write the next chapter. What will your story be?

10 EPILOGUE

WRITING YOUR OWN SUCCESS STORY

As you go through this book, take a moment to reflect. You've walked through stories of struggle, frustration, and incredible triumph. You've seen people hit rock bottom, face impossible odds, and come out on the other side stronger, wiser, and wealthier. But here's the truth: their stories aren't just about them—they're about you.

Maybe you see a bit of yourself in Mike, who had to start over from scratch. Or in Jessica, who shifted her mindset and unlocked the abundance she never thought possible. Maybe you've felt the sting of failure like David, or the joy of discovering your niche like Lisa. Perhaps you're inspired by Haley's brand-building journey or Sam's tech-driven growth. Or maybe Tyler's realization that true success is about giving back hit close to home. And then there's Caroline, who reminded us all that sustaining success requires constant evolution.

But these stories are just one part of the equation. The other part? That's you. Your journey. Your dreams. Your challenges.

UNSTOPPABLE

Think about where you are right now. Are you feeling stuck, frustrated, or unsure of the next step? Or maybe you're already on your way, but you're wondering how to take it further, how to make it last. Whatever your situation, remember this: You have the power to write your own success story. And it doesn't have to follow anyone else's script.

Success isn't reserved for the lucky few. It's not something that only happens to other people. It's something you can create, one step at a time, starting right now.

Let's be real—it won't be easy. There will be days when you want to quit, when everything seems too hard, too overwhelming. But that's when you have to dig deep, remember the stories you've read, and keep pushing forward. Because the truth is, every successful person you admire has faced those same doubts, those same fears. What sets them apart is that they didn't let those doubts stop them. And you don't have to either.

So, where do you start? Start with a mindset shift. Stop telling yourself what you can't do, and start focusing on what you can. Look for opportunities where others see obstacles. Embrace failure as a learning experience, not a dead end. And most importantly, never lose sight of your passion, your purpose, your "why."

UNSTOPPABLE

Next, take action. Even the smallest step forward is progress. Whether it's starting that side hustle you've been thinking about, finally taking the leap into entrepreneurship, or simply setting aside time each day to work on your goals—just start. Momentum builds with action, and before you know it, those small steps will turn into giant leaps.

But don't forget to give back along the way. Success isn't just about what you achieve; it's about how you use it to make a difference. Whether it's helping a friend, mentoring someone who's just starting out, or investing in your community—find ways to pay it forward. It's one of the most rewarding parts of the journey.

And finally, keep evolving. Success isn't a one-time event; it's a continuous process. Stay curious, stay adaptable, and always be willing to learn. The world is constantly changing, and the only way to stay on top is to change with it.

As you move forward, remember that your story is yours to write. There's no right or wrong way to do it—there's only your way. The journey won't always be smooth, and it won't always be easy. But it will be worth it. Because in the end, success isn't just about reaching a destination—it's about the person you become along the way.

So, as you reach this far, I want to leave you with one thought: The next chapter is up to you. The ideas, the tools, the inspiration—they're all here. Now it's your turn to take them and run with them, to create a life that's not just successful, but meaningful, fulfilling, and uniquely yours.

You've got this. Your story is just beginning, and I can't wait to see where it takes you.

Now go out there and write the best damn story of your life.

THE ROAD LESS TRAVELED

EMBRACING THE UNEXPECTED PATH TO WEALTH

Not every success story follows a straight line. Sometimes, the path to wealth and fulfillment is winding, filled with unexpected detours and surprising turns. It's the road less traveled, the one that most people overlook because it doesn't look like the "traditional" route to success. But often, it's on this road where the most extraordinary stories are born.

That's exactly what happened to Casey. Casey was the kind of person who always played it safe. Growing up, she followed the rules, got good grades, and did everything she was supposed to do. She went to college, got a stable job in finance, and settled into a comfortable routine. On paper, everything looked perfect—good salary, nice apartment, and a future that seemed secure.

But there was something gnawing at her. Every morning, as she sipped her coffee and prepared for another day at the office, she felt a quiet dissatisfaction growing inside her. The job that had once excited her now felt suffocating, and the career she had worked so hard to build seemed more like a trap than a triumph. She was restless, but she didn't know why—or what to do about it.

Then, one day, life threw her a curveball. Out of nowhere, Casey's company announced massive layoffs, and she was one of the first to go. Just like that, her sense of security was shattered. She was devastated, angry, and scared. How could this happen after all her hard work? What was she supposed to do now?

UNSTOPPABLE

The days that followed were some of the darkest Casey had ever faced. She felt lost, like everything she had worked for had been ripped away. She applied for jobs, went to interviews, but nothing seemed to click. The rejection emails started piling up, and with each one, her confidence took another hit. For the first time in her life, Casey didn't have a plan.

But then, something unexpected happened. With nothing left to lose, Casey started doing something she hadn't done in years—she picked up her camera. Photography had always been a hobby of hers, something she loved but never took seriously. But now, with all this free time on her hands, she found herself drawn to it more and more. She started taking long walks around the city, capturing moments that spoke to her, finding beauty in the ordinary.

At first, it was just a way to pass the time, a distraction from the stress and uncertainty. But the more she did it, the more she realized how much she loved it—how much she needed it. Photography gave her a sense of purpose, a way to express herself that her corporate job never had. It was like a light had been turned on inside her, illuminating a passion she had buried for years.

UNSTOPPABLE

Friends began to notice her work and encouraged her to share it online. Hesitant at first, Casey started posting her photos on social media, and to her surprise, they quickly gained traction. People loved her unique perspective, the way she captured the world around her. She began to build a following, and soon, strangers were reaching out, asking if they could buy prints or hire her for photo shoots.

It was a turning point. Casey realized that maybe, just maybe, she didn't need to go back to the corporate world. Maybe she could turn this unexpected passion into something real, something that could support her financially and fulfill her creatively. It was a risky move, but for the first time in a long time, Casey felt alive—like she was finally on the path she was meant to take.

So, she went for it. She invested in better equipment, took online courses to hone her skills, and started marketing herself as a professional photographer. It wasn't easy—there were times when she wondered if she had made a mistake, when the bills were piling up and the work wasn't coming in fast enough. But she stuck with it, determined to make it work.

And slowly but surely, it did. Casey's photography business began to grow. She landed gigs with local businesses, started getting featured in online publications, and even had her work displayed in a few galleries. Her social media following exploded, and before long, she was making more money from photography than she ever had in her corporate job. But more than the money, it was the fulfillment that kept her going—the knowledge that she was doing something she loved, something that mattered to her.

Today, Casey is a successful photographer with a thriving business and a life that she never could have imagined back in her cubicle. She's traveled the world, met incredible people, and created a body of work that she's truly proud of. And it all started with a layoff—a moment that seemed like the end but was really just the beginning of a new, unexpected journey.

Casey's story is a testament to the power of embracing the unexpected. Sometimes, the path to success isn't the one you plan for. Sometimes, it's the one that finds you when everything else falls apart. The road less traveled can be scary, uncertain, and full of challenges, but it's also where you'll find the most growth, the most fulfillment, and the most surprising rewards.

So, if you find yourself facing a setback, a detour, or an unexpected change in your life, don't be afraid to explore where it might lead you. Maybe there's a passion you've been ignoring, a talent you've been downplaying, or a dream you've been too scared to chase. This could be your chance to take the road less traveled—to turn a moment of frustration into the start of something incredible.

Remember, success doesn't always look the way you expect it to. Sometimes, it's about following your heart, taking risks, and being open to the possibilities that life throws your way. Casey found her true path not by sticking to the plan, but by embracing the detour. And you can, too.

As you close this final chapter, take a moment to think about your own journey. What unexpected paths might be waiting for you? What passions are you ready to explore? The road ahead might be uncertain, but it's also full of potential. So go out there, take the leap, and see where the road less traveled might take you.

Because the most amazing success stories are the ones you never saw coming. And yours might be just around the corner.

EMBRACING THE UNKNOWN

THE MILLIONAIRE MINDSET

Let's talk about fear. Not the jump-scare kind of fear, but the deep, gut-wrenching fear that comes when you're standing on the edge of something big, something life-changing. It's the fear of the unknown, the fear of failure, the fear that maybe—just maybe—you're not cut out for the dreams you've been daring to dream.

Jake knew that fear all too well. On the surface, Jake was living the dream. He had a steady job, a nice apartment, and a life that looked pretty damn good from the outside. But inside, Jake was struggling. Every day felt like a battle against the clock, against the monotony, against the nagging feeling that he was meant for more. He couldn't shake the sense that his life was slipping away, that he was missing out on something greater, something that could bring real meaning and fulfillment.

Jake had always been fascinated by technology. As a kid, he spent hours tinkering with computers, taking them apart just to see how they worked, then putting them back together. It was his passion, his escape, and as he got older, he dreamed of creating something—an app, a startup, something that could make a real impact. But the fear was always there, holding him back. What if it failed? What if he lost everything? What if he just wasn't good enough?

UNSTOPPABLE

So, Jake did what so many of us do—he played it safe. He kept his tech dreams on the back burner, convincing himself that someday he'd take the leap, someday he'd go for it. But that day never seemed to come. There was always a reason to wait—another promotion, another raise, another year of saving up for that elusive "right moment."

Then, everything changed in an instant. Jake's company announced a merger, and just like that, his department was downsized. He was out of a job, out of the security he'd clung to for so long, and left with nothing but his fears staring him in the face. But as the initial shock wore off, Jake realized something—this was his moment. The safety net was gone, and for the first time, he was free to chase the dreams he'd been too scared to pursue.

With nothing to lose, Jake threw himself into his passion. He dusted off old notebooks filled with app ideas, scribbled new ones, and started coding like a man possessed. Days turned into nights, and nights into early mornings, but Jake didn't care. He was alive in a way he hadn't been in years, fueled by a mix of fear and excitement, uncertainty, and hope.

UNSTOPPABLE

But it wasn't easy. The doubts crept in, the fear of failure nagged at him, and there were moments when he wondered if he'd made a huge mistake. Money was tight, the bills were piling up, and the job offers he'd turned down started looking pretty tempting. But every time he thought about giving up, he remembered how it felt to live someone else's version of success—how empty it had been, how unfulfilled he'd felt. So, he kept going.

And then, one day, it happened. Jake's app launched. It wasn't perfect, and it didn't take off overnight, but it caught the attention of a small but passionate group of users. Word spread, and soon, what had started as a late-night coding project began to grow into something real. Investors started calling, opportunities opened up, and before he knew it, Jake was running his own tech company—a company built on his passion, his vision, and his willingness to embrace the unknown.

Jake's story is about more than just starting a business. It's about facing your fears head-on, about daring to leap into the unknown even when everything inside you is screaming to play it safe. It's about recognizing that the only thing standing between you and the life you want is the fear of failure. And here's the truth: that fear never really goes away. But you learn to live with it, to let it push you forward instead of holding you back.

The millionaire mindset isn't just about making money—it's about making bold moves, about taking risks, about trusting yourself even when the path ahead isn't clear. It's about knowing that failure is part of the process, not the end of the road. And it's about understanding that the greatest rewards come when you're willing to step outside your comfort zone and embrace the unknown.

So, as you close this book and step back into your life, remember Jake's story. Remember that the fear you feel is normal, that the doubts are just part of the journey. But also remember that the life you want is on the other side of that fear. It's waiting for you, ready to be claimed, ready to be lived.

Your path won't look like anyone else's, and that's okay. It's not supposed to. Success isn't about following someone else's blueprint—it's about creating your own. It's about finding the courage to pursue your passions, to take risks, to fail, and to try again.

So, what's your next move? What's the dream you've been too scared to chase? The idea you've been sitting on, the passion you've been ignoring? Now's the time. Now's your moment.

Step into the unknown. Embrace the fear. And start writing the next chapter of your success story—because the only thing standing between you and your dreams is the belief that you can do it.

And you can. You absolutely can.

THE TURNING POINT

WHEN EVERYTHING CHANGES

There's a moment in every success story that changes everything. It's the turning point, the fork in the road where you have to make a choice: keep playing it safe or take a risk that could redefine your life. But here's the thing—they don't always come with a big announcement. Sometimes, they're wrapped in pain, frustration, and the kind of soul-crushing doubt that makes you question everything. This is the story of Amanda, and how her darkest moment became the catalyst for something extraordinary.

Amanda had always been a dreamer. From a young age, she wanted more than the ordinary, more than what she saw around her growing up in a small Midwestern town. Her parents were hardworking, decent people, but they lived paycheck to paycheck, always scraping by. Amanda swore that one day, she would break free from that cycle. She wanted to see the world, to live in a way that didn't involve counting pennies and making do.

But life, as it often does, had other plans. Amanda got a scholarship to a good college and graduated with honors, full of hope and ambition. But after college, reality hit hard. The economy wasn't great, and despite her degree, the only job she could find was as a receptionist at a small insurance company. It was a far cry from the dreams she had nurtured, but she told herself it was just a stepping stone, a temporary stop on the way to something bigger.

UNSTOPPABLE

But years passed, and that bigger something never came. The job was secure but unfulfilling, the pay was steady but never enough to get ahead. Amanda watched as friends got promoted, started businesses, moved to big cities, and chased their dreams. She felt like she was stuck in place, her life a series of monotonous days that blended into one another.

It wasn't just about the job. It was about everything. Amanda had always imagined her life would be different—filled with adventure, passion, and purpose. But instead, she felt trapped in a routine that was slowly suffocating her. She went through the motions, but inside, she was crumbling. The dreams she had once held so close felt more and more out of reach, and she couldn't shake the growing sense of failure that shadowed her every step.

Then came the day that broke her. It was a Wednesday, not unlike any other, but for Amanda, it was the day everything came crashing down. Her boss, a man who had never really seen her potential, called her into his office and told her that the company was downsizing. Her position was being eliminated, effective immediately. Just like that, the small bit of stability she'd clung to was gone.

UNSTOPPABLE

Amanda walked out of the office in a daze, her thoughts a jumble of fear and anger. She drove home, sat on her couch, and for the first time in years, let herself cry. The weight of everything she had been holding in—the frustration, the disappointment, the fear of never becoming who she wanted to be—came pouring out.

But after the tears dried, something unexpected happened. Sitting there in the quiet of her tiny apartment, Amanda felt a strange sense of clarity. It was as if losing her job had stripped away the last layer of safety, leaving her with nothing but the raw truth: she was at rock bottom. But for the first time, she realized that rock bottom wasn't the end. It was a beginning. A blank slate. A chance to rebuild, to do things differently, to finally chase the dreams she had been too scared to pursue.

Amanda made a decision that day. She wasn't going to look for another job, another safe but unfulfilling position. She was going to take a chance on herself, on the dreams she had buried for too long. Amanda had always been passionate about writing. In college, she had written stories, articles, even a blog that had gained a small following. But she had never dared to think she could make a living from it. Now, with nothing left to lose, she decided to try.

UNSTOPPABLE

She started freelancing, picking up small gigs online—writing blog posts, editing content, anything she could get her hands on. The pay was meager at first, and there were days when she questioned her decision, when the fear crept back in, whispering that she was making a mistake. But Amanda pushed through, fueled by the determination that had once driven her dreams.

Slowly, things began to change. Her clients loved her work, and word spread. She started getting bigger projects, better opportunities. Amanda found herself writing for major publications, crafting content for well-known brands, and building a portfolio that was both impressive and rewarding. Her income grew, but more importantly, so did her confidence. For the first time, she was doing something she loved, something that made her feel alive.

But Amanda didn't stop there. She had always wanted to write a book, a novel that had been simmering in the back of her mind for years. With her newfound success, she decided to go for it. She wrote every day, pouring her heart into the story that had been waiting to be told. It wasn't easy, and there were plenty of nights when she wondered if anyone would ever read it, but she kept going.

UNSTOPPABLE

When the book was finally finished, Amanda self-published it, unsure of what would happen next. She didn't have big expectations—just a hope that maybe a few people would connect with it. But then, something incredible happened. The book took off. It resonated with readers in a way she had never imagined. It climbed the charts, got glowing reviews, and before she knew it, Amanda was a bestselling author.

The girl who had once felt like a failure, trapped in a life she didn't want, had become a success story. But more than the money or the recognition, it was the fulfillment that mattered most. Amanda had found her purpose, her passion, and the courage to chase it. And it all started on the day she lost everything.

Amanda's story is a powerful reminder that sometimes, the turning points in our lives come when we least expect them. They don't always look like opportunities at first—often, they're wrapped in loss, in pain, in the kind of fear that makes you want to run in the other direction. But those moments, when everything seems to be falling apart, are often the ones that lead to the greatest breakthroughs.

UNSTOPPABLE

So, if you're facing a turning point in your life, if you're standing at a crossroads wondering what to do next, remember Amanda's story. Remember that the path to success isn't always straight, and it's not always easy. But if you're willing to take a chance, to embrace the uncertainty and push through the fear, you might just find that the life you've always wanted is waiting for you on the other side.

The road ahead may be unknown, but that's where the magic happens. That's where dreams are born, where success is forged, and where you become the person you were always meant to be.

So take the leap. Embrace the turning point. And watch as your life transforms in ways you never imagined.

This is your moment. What will you do with it?

UNSTOPPABLE

THE POWER OF A SINGLE YES

14

WHEN EVERYTHING CHANGES

Sometimes, all it takes is one moment, one decision, one word, to change your life forever. That's what happened to Ben. His story is a testament to the fact that you're often just one "yes" away from turning your entire life around. But to get to that yes, you have to go through a lot of no's, and a lot of hard days where giving up feels like the only option.

Ben was no stranger to hard work. He'd grown up in a small town where opportunities were scarce, but dreams were big. He had always wanted more for himself, something beyond the factory jobs that everyone else seemed to end up in. After high school, Ben took a leap of faith and moved to the city, determined to make something of himself. He didn't know exactly what that would be, but he was ready to hustle, ready to do whatever it took.

He started out like so many others—working odd jobs, barely scraping by, and always on the lookout for the next big opportunity. Ben knew he had the drive, but every time he thought he was getting close, something would knock him back. The promising job interview that ended with a polite rejection. The startup idea that fell apart when his partner backed out. The countless nights spent working late, only to realize that he was still miles away from where he wanted to be.

UNSTOPPABLE

But Ben kept going. He didn't know how to quit, even when it felt like the world was telling him to. He was exhausted, frustrated, and sometimes, downright defeated. But deep down, there was a fire that wouldn't go out, a belief that somehow, some way, his break was coming.

Then came the moment that changed everything.

One day, while scrolling through job listings, Ben came across a posting for a sales position at a small tech company. It wasn't glamorous, and it wasn't exactly what he'd dreamed of, but something about it caught his eye. Maybe it was the challenge, maybe it was the possibility of getting his foot in the door of an industry that was booming, or maybe it was just that he needed a win. Whatever it was, he applied.

To his surprise, he got a callback. The interview was tough—grueling, even. The hiring manager grilled him on his lack of experience, questioned his ability to handle the pressure, and made it clear that this job wasn't for the faint of heart. But Ben didn't back down. He told them why he was the right person for the job, why he was willing to work harder than anyone else, why he was hungry for the opportunity.

UNSTOPPABLE

When the interview was over, Ben walked out of the building with mixed feelings. He felt like he'd given it his all, but doubt was gnawing at him. What if it wasn't enough? What if this was just another "no" in a long line of rejections?

The next day, Ben got the call. He braced himself for the worst, ready to hear those familiar words—"We've decided to go with someone else." But instead, he heard something that made his heart skip a beat.

"We'd like to offer you the position."

That one "yes" changed everything. Ben threw himself into the job with everything he had. It wasn't easy—there were long hours, steep learning curves, and plenty of moments where he wondered if he was in over his head. But Ben thrived under the pressure. He learned fast, hustled harder than anyone else, and started closing deals that made people take notice.

Within a year, Ben had moved from being the new guy to one of the top performers in the company. He didn't just hit his targets; he shattered them. He brought in big clients, made big commissions, and started to build a reputation as the guy who could get things done. His bosses took notice, and soon, Ben was promoted, given more responsibility, more opportunities, and more money than he'd ever imagined.

UNSTOPPABLE

But the real turning point came when one of the company's biggest investors pulled him aside after a meeting. He'd been watching Ben's rise, impressed by his work ethic, his results, and his ability to close deals. The investor made Ben an offer: a chance to join a new venture he was backing—a tech startup with huge potential.

It was a risk, no doubt about it. Ben would have to leave the security of his job, the steady paycheck, the success he had worked so hard for. But he knew this was the moment he had been waiting for, the chance to take everything he'd learned and apply it to something that could be truly life-changing.

So, he said yes.

That single decision, that single "yes," catapulted Ben into a new world. The startup took off, and with Ben at the helm of the sales team, it quickly became one of the fastest-growing companies in the industry. He wasn't just making a living anymore—he was building a legacy. When the company went public a few years later, Ben's shares made him a millionaire overnight.

UNSTOPPABLE

Ben's story isn't just about making money. It's about perseverance, about pushing through the hard times, the rejections, the moments of doubt, and never giving up on yourself. It's about recognizing that sometimes, all you need is that one yes to change your life forever.

If you're in a place right now where it feels like the world keeps saying no, if you're tired, frustrated, and wondering when your break is going to come, remember Ben's story. Remember that you're just one yes away from everything changing. But you have to keep going, keep showing up, keep believing that your moment is coming.

Because it is.

The road to success is rarely a straight line. It's full of twists, turns, and unexpected detours. But it's those moments—the ones that challenge you, push you, make you question everything—that often lead to the greatest rewards.

So keep pushing. Keep believing. Your "yes" is out there, waiting for you. And when it comes, it will change everything.
Are you ready for it?

THE BREAKTHROUGH

TURNING PAIN INTO PROFIT

Let's talk about rock bottom. That place where it feels like the walls are closing in, where every move you make seems to push you further down instead of lifting you up. It's a place most people fear, a place no one wants to visit. But sometimes, it's exactly where you need to be to see things clearly, to find the fire that will fuel your rise. This is the story of Rachel, who hit rock bottom and found her way out, not just to survive, but to thrive in ways she never thought possible.

Rachel was always the one with a plan. She was the kind of person who mapped out her life in five-year increments, with goals, deadlines, and backup plans for every scenario. She did everything right—graduated with honors, landed a good job in a corporate setting, and even bought a small house by the time she was 28. On paper, she was living the dream. But life has a funny way of throwing curveballs when you least expect them.

For Rachel, that curveball came in the form of a layoff. The company she worked for merged with a larger corporation, and suddenly, her department was deemed redundant. Just like that, her stable, well-planned life was upended. She went from having a solid career path to staring at an empty inbox, no job prospects in sight, and bills that weren't going to wait.

UNSTOPPABLE

At first, Rachel tried to stay positive. She threw herself into job hunting, applying for every position that remotely matched her skills. But weeks turned into months, and the rejection emails piled up. The longer she went without a job, the more the doubt started to creep in. She began to question everything—her skills, her choices, her worth. The confidence that had always been her foundation started to crumble.

Rachel's savings dwindled, and soon, she was struggling to make ends meet. The stress was overwhelming. She cut back on everything, trying to stretch every dollar, but it wasn't enough. She fell behind on her mortgage, and for the first time in her life, she was truly scared—scared of losing her home, scared of losing herself.

Then came the day that broke her. She was sitting at her kitchen table, surrounded by bills she couldn't pay, when she got a call from the bank. They were starting foreclosure proceedings on her house. Rachel felt the world drop out from under her. She hung up the phone and just sat there, numb. This was rock bottom, and she had no idea how to climb out.

But sometimes, rock bottom is where you find your true strength. After the initial shock wore off, Rachel realized she had two choices: she could let this situation defeat her, or she could fight like hell to change it. And Rachel was a fighter.

UNSTOPPABLE

She knew she needed to do something drastic, something that would turn her situation around. That's when she remembered a small side project she had started years ago—making and selling homemade skincare products. It was something she did for fun, something that brought her joy in the midst of her busy life. She had always gotten great feedback from friends and family, but she never thought it could be more than just a hobby.

With nothing left to lose, Rachel decided to go all in. She spent her last bit of savings on supplies, turned her kitchen into a makeshift lab, and started crafting her products with a renewed sense of purpose. She set up a website, created social media accounts, and began marketing her skincare line with the little knowledge she had picked up from online courses.

At first, it was slow going. Sales trickled in, just enough to keep her going, but not enough to make a real dent in her financial situation. But Rachel was determined. She reached out to local boutiques, pitched her products at farmers' markets, and sent samples to influencers she admired. She worked around the clock, driven by the need to pull herself out of the hole she was in.

UNSTOPPABLE

Then, something amazing happened. One of the influencers she had sent samples to—a well-known beauty blogger with a massive following—posted a glowing review of Rachel's products. Overnight, Rachel's website blew up. Orders started pouring in from all over the country, and she could barely keep up with the demand. Her little side project had turned into a full-blown business, and it was taking off in a way she had never imagined.

Rachel's skincare line became a sensation. Customers loved the quality, the story behind the brand, and the fact that it was created by someone who truly cared about what she was making. Rachel expanded her product line, hired a small team to help with production, and within a year, her business was generating more income than her corporate job ever had.

But more than the financial success, it was the personal transformation that mattered most. Rachel had gone from feeling like a failure to realizing that she was capable of so much more than she had ever given herself credit for. She had taken the worst moment of her life and turned it into something beautiful, something that brought value not just to her, but to her customers as well.

UNSTOPPABLE

Rachel's story is a powerful reminder that sometimes, the thing that seems like the end is really just the beginning. Rock bottom isn't a place to be feared—it's a place where you can strip away everything that doesn't matter and find out what you're really made of. It's where you can dig deep, find your passion, and build something incredible from the ground up.

If you're facing your own rock bottom moment right now, remember Rachel's story. Remember that the pain, the frustration, the fear—they don't define you. What defines you is what you do next. Will you let it break you, or will you use it as the fuel to create something amazing?

The road to success is rarely smooth. It's full of twists, turns, and unexpected challenges. But it's those very challenges that shape you, that force you to grow, and that ultimately lead you to the breakthrough you've been waiting for.

So, if you're at rock bottom, know this: you have the power to turn it around. You have the strength to rise, to build, to succeed. And when you do, your story will be one that inspires others to do the same.

Because success isn't just about the destination—it's about the journey, and the person you become along the way.

Your breakthrough is waiting. Go find it.

THE PIVOT

WHEN LIFE FORCES A CHANGE OF PLANS

Sometimes, life has a way of pulling the rug out from under you, leaving you scrambling to figure out your next move. You've got everything mapped out, and then—bam!—something unexpected happens, and suddenly your plans are in shambles. It's in these moments that you have to make a choice: do you cling to the life you thought you were supposed to have, or do you pivot and create something entirely new?

That's exactly the choice Logan faced when his world turned upside down.

Logan was living the life he'd always dreamed of. He was a rising star in the advertising world, working at a top agency in New York City. His days were filled with high-profile clients, creative campaigns, and the kind of hustle that made him feel alive. He loved the energy, the fast pace, and the feeling that he was on the cutting edge of something big. At just 32, Logan was on track to becoming one of the youngest partners in the agency's history.

But then, everything changed.

UNSTOPPABLE

It started with a pain in his chest—a tightness that he brushed off as stress. After all, Logan was used to working long hours, running on coffee and adrenaline, and sacrificing sleep for success. But the pain didn't go away. In fact, it got worse. One night, after another grueling day at the office, Logan collapsed in his apartment. The next thing he knew, he was waking up in a hospital bed, his body hooked up to machines, doctors standing over him with serious faces.

Logan had suffered a heart attack. At 32 years old, he had pushed himself so hard that his body couldn't take it anymore. The doctors told him he was lucky to be alive, that if he didn't make some major changes, the next time might not have such a happy ending. They advised him to slow down, to find balance, to rethink his priorities.

For Logan, it was a wake-up call like no other. Lying in that hospital bed, he realized that the life he had been chasing was slowly killing him. The success, the money, the status—it had all come at a cost, and now he was paying the price. He knew he couldn't go back to the way things were, but the idea of leaving behind the career he had worked so hard to build terrified him. Who was he if he wasn't the hotshot ad executive? What would he do if he wasn't running at full speed every day?

UNSTOPPABLE

After he was discharged from the hospital, Logan took some time off to recover. At first, he didn't know what to do with himself. The silence was deafening, and the lack of structure left him feeling lost. But slowly, he began to rediscover parts of himself that he had buried under years of nonstop work. He started cooking, something he hadn't done since college. He took up photography, capturing the beauty of the city at sunrise, a time of day he had never seen because he was always asleep or already at the office.

It was during one of these quiet mornings, standing on the Brooklyn Bridge with his camera, that Logan had an idea—a simple thought that would change everything. What if he could combine his love for creativity with his need for a healthier, more balanced life? What if he could create something new, something that allowed him to use his skills without sacrificing his well-being?

Logan decided to pivot. He left the high-stakes world of advertising and started his own boutique creative agency, one that focused on working with wellness brands, local businesses, and startups that shared his values of balance, health, and sustainability. It was a risky move—he was walking away from a stable, high-paying job to start something from scratch. But for the first time in a long time, Logan felt like he was on the right path.

UNSTOPPABLE

The early days were tough. He had to rebuild his client base, learn the ins and outs of running a business, and prove himself all over again. But Logan approached it with the same passion and drive that had fueled his career before, only this time, he did it on his own terms. He worked with clients he believed in, took on projects that excited him, and made time for the things that truly mattered—his health, his relationships, his life outside of work.

And the results were nothing short of amazing. Logan's agency quickly gained a reputation for its fresh, innovative approach to marketing. Clients loved the personal attention, the creative solutions, and the fact that Logan brought the same big-agency expertise without the big-agency attitude. Word spread, and before long, his small boutique agency was thriving, pulling in big-name clients who appreciated his unique vision.

But more than the financial success, Logan found something he hadn't even realized he was missing—fulfillment. He was doing work that mattered to him, work that aligned with his values and his vision for the life he wanted to live. He was making a difference, not just in his clients' businesses, but in his own life as well. He had found balance, a way to be successful without sacrificing his health or his happiness.

Logan's story is a powerful reminder that sometimes, life forces you to pivot. It's easy to get caught up in a vision of success that's based on someone else's definition, but when the universe throws you a curveball, it's an opportunity to redefine what success means for you. It's a chance to step back, reassess, and create a life that's not just about achieving goals, but about living in a way that's sustainable, fulfilling, and true to who you are.

So, if you're feeling like life is pushing you in a new direction, if circumstances are forcing you to rethink your plans, don't be afraid to pivot. Don't be afraid to let go of what's no longer serving you and embrace the unknown. The path may be uncertain, but it's also full of potential.

Remember, success isn't just about reaching a destination—it's about how you get there. It's about being open to change, being willing to take risks, and being brave enough to forge a new path when the old one no longer fits.

Logan found his true calling not by sticking to the plan, but by pivoting when life forced his hand. And in doing so, he created a life that was richer, more meaningful, and more fulfilling than anything he had imagined.

You can do the same. Trust the process, embrace the pivot, and watch as your life transforms in ways you never thought possible.

Your next chapter is waiting. What will you do with it?

17

THE REDEMPTION

REBUILDING FROM RUIN

Everyone loves a good comeback story. There's something powerful about watching someone rise from the ashes, reclaim their life, and find success where there was once only failure. But the road to redemption isn't easy. It's paved with pain, regret, and hard lessons that most people would rather avoid. This is the story of Marcus, a man who lost everything, only to find that sometimes, losing it all is the first step toward gaining what really matters.

Marcus had always been a high achiever. He was the kind of guy who seemed to have everything figured out—top of his class in college, a fast-track career in finance, and a lifestyle that most people only dream of. By the time he was 30, Marcus was living in a penthouse apartment, driving a luxury car, and rubbing shoulders with the city's elite. He was on top of the world, and he made sure everyone knew it.

But behind the flashy exterior, Marcus was struggling. The pressure to maintain his success, to keep up the image he had built, was crushing. He was working insane hours, barely sleeping, and numbing himself with whatever he could find to keep the stress at bay. On the outside, he looked like he was living the dream, but on the inside, he was unraveling.

Then came the crash.

UNSTOPPABLE

Marcus had taken a big gamble—a risky investment that he was sure would pay off in a big way. He had leveraged everything he had, betting it all on a deal that looked like a sure thing. But the market turned against him, and within days, everything he had worked for came crashing down. He lost millions, not just his money but other people's money, too—clients, friends, people who had trusted him. The fallout was brutal. Lawsuits, public humiliation, and a reputation in ruins. Marcus went from being the golden boy of finance to a pariah overnight.

In the blink of an eye, Marcus lost everything—his job, his wealth, his friends, even his health. The stress and shame took a toll on him, and he found himself alone in a hospital bed, suffering from a heart attack brought on by the relentless pressure he had been under. He was 32, bankrupt, and utterly broken.

For months, Marcus didn't know how to move forward. The life he had built was gone, and he couldn't see a way out. He had hit rock bottom, and the guilt and regret were eating him alive. He isolated himself, cut off contact with the few people who still cared, and sank into a deep depression. There were days when he wondered if he would ever find a way back, or if this was how his story would end.

UNSTOPPABLE

But rock bottom has a way of forcing you to confront the truth. As the days turned into weeks, Marcus realized that he had been living a lie. The success he had chased so desperately had been hollow, built on ego and the need for validation. He had lost sight of who he was, what he really valued, and what he wanted his life to be about.

One night, sitting in his darkened apartment, Marcus made a decision. He was done with the facade, done with the chase for status and wealth. He knew he had to start over, but this time, he would do it differently. He would rebuild, not just his finances, but his life—based on honesty, integrity, and a true sense of purpose.

The first step was making amends. Marcus reached out to everyone he had hurt, everyone who had lost money because of his mistakes. He apologized, not just for the financial loss, but for the arrogance and greed that had driven him. Some forgave him, others didn't, but Marcus knew it was a step he had to take to move forward.

Next, he focused on his health. He started exercising, eating right, and seeing a therapist to deal with the emotional scars that had been buried for too long. It was a slow process, and there were setbacks, but Marcus was determined to heal, both physically and mentally.

UNSTOPPABLE

As he began to regain his strength, Marcus started thinking about his next move. He knew he couldn't go back to the world of finance—not in the same way. The idea of chasing after money and status made him sick. But he also knew he had valuable skills, skills that could be used for something good.

That's when he had an idea—what if he used his experience, both the successes and the failures, to help others? What if he could teach people how to manage their money wisely, how to build wealth without losing their soul in the process? What if he could turn his biggest mistake into a way to give back?

Marcus decided to start small. He began offering free financial workshops at community centers, teaching basic budgeting, saving, and investing skills to people who needed it most. He didn't charge a dime—he was doing it for the love of helping others, for the chance to make a positive impact.

Word spread quickly. People who attended his workshops told their friends, who told their friends, and soon, Marcus was being asked to speak at events, to consult for nonprofits, to help small businesses get off the ground. His passion for helping others reignited something in him, something he hadn't felt in years—true fulfillment.

But it didn't stop there. As Marcus's reputation as a financial educator grew, he started receiving offers from companies and investors who wanted to support his mission. They believed in what he was doing, and they wanted to help him reach more people. Marcus founded a nonprofit organization dedicated to financial literacy, focusing on underserved communities and those who had been hit hardest by economic downturns.

Within a few years, Marcus's organization had expanded nationwide, offering workshops, online courses, and one-on-one coaching. He was invited to speak at conferences, featured in media outlets, and recognized for his work in transforming lives through financial education. But this time, the success felt different. It wasn't about ego or status—it was about making a real difference.

Marcus had rebuilt his life, not by chasing after what he had lost, but by finding a new purpose, a new way to use his talents to help others. He had turned his biggest failure into his greatest success, and in doing so, he had found a sense of peace and fulfillment that had eluded him during his years at the top.

His story is a powerful reminder that redemption is always possible, that it's never too late to turn your life around. No matter how far you've fallen, no matter how many mistakes you've made, there's always a way forward—if you're willing to face the truth, make amends, and rebuild with integrity and purpose.

UNSTOPPABLE

If you're facing your own dark night of the soul, if you're wondering how you'll ever recover from the mistakes you've made, remember Marcus's story. Remember that rock bottom isn't the end—it's the beginning of a new chapter, one where you have the power to redefine your life on your terms.

You can rise from the ashes. You can rebuild. And when you do, your story of redemption will be one that inspires others to believe in the possibility of their own comeback.

The world loves a good comeback story. Maybe it's time to start writing yours.

18

FINDING GOLD WHERE OTHERS SEE DIRT

Opportunity often comes disguised as hard work, frustration, or even failure. It's easy to miss, especially when you're caught up in the grind of everyday life. But sometimes, the thing that everyone else overlooks, dismisses, or complains about is the very thing that could change your life forever. This is the story of Ethan, who found his million-dollar idea in a place where most people only saw problems.

Ethan was your average guy—nothing fancy, nothing flashy. He grew up in a small town where everyone knew everyone, went to the local state college, and landed a job at a local warehouse right after graduation. The job was decent, steady, but far from exciting. He spent his days managing inventory, moving boxes, and dealing with the occasional shipping mishap. It was the kind of job that paid the bills but left little room for dreaming.

Ethan wasn't unhappy, but he wasn't exactly fulfilled either. He knew there had to be more to life than clocking in and out every day, but he didn't know what that "more" looked like. He had no grand vision, no burning passion, just a vague feeling that he was meant for something else. But without a clear direction, he stayed put, day after day, watching the years slip by.

Then, one particularly grueling week, everything seemed to go wrong. A major supplier botched an order, leaving Ethan's warehouse with thousands of the wrong products. Customers were furious, returns were piling up, and the stress was through the roof. Ethan found himself working overtime, trying to sort out the mess, dealing with angry phone calls, and feeling the weight of the world on his shoulders.

One night, exhausted and frustrated, Ethan sat down in the break room with a cup of bad coffee and thought about his life. Was this it? Was this all there was? He felt like he was stuck in a never-ending cycle of problems that weren't even his fault. But as he sat there, staring at the stacks of returned boxes, something clicked.

What if these problems could be an opportunity?

Ethan started thinking about all the returned products—perfectly good items that couldn't be resold as new because of minor packaging issues or small defects. The warehouse was overflowing with them, and they were costing the company a fortune in lost revenue and storage fees. Most of these items would end up being sold off in bulk for pennies on the dollar, or worse, thrown away entirely.

But what if, instead of seeing them as a problem, he could turn them into a solution? What if there was a way to sell these products directly to consumers at a discount, turning waste into profit? It wasn't a glamorous idea, but it was a practical one—and the more Ethan thought about it, the more he realized it had potential.

He decided to test the waters. On his own time, Ethan started researching online marketplaces, learning about how other businesses sold overstock, returned, or slightly damaged goods. He noticed that there was a growing demand for discounted items, especially among bargain hunters who didn't mind a dinged box or a minor flaw if it meant saving money.

Ethan pitched his idea to his boss—a simple, no-nonsense proposal to set up an online store where the warehouse could sell these products directly to consumers at a discount. At first, his boss was skeptical. It seemed like a lot of work for something that might not pay off. But Ethan was persistent. He showed him the numbers, the potential savings, the possibility of turning a loss into a profit. Eventually, his boss agreed to give it a try.

They started small. Ethan set up a basic website, took photos of the returned products, and listed them online with honest descriptions of their condition. The prices were low, the margins were slim, but the goal was simple: turn waste into revenue.

And then, the orders started coming in.

Slowly at first, then more steadily. People loved the deals, and word began to spread. Ethan expanded the inventory, adding more products, improving the website, and handling customer service himself. The operation grew, and within months, it was generating significant revenue—enough to catch the attention of the higher-ups at the company.

What had started as a side project, a simple idea born out of frustration, quickly became a full-fledged business. The company invested more resources into it, allowing Ethan to hire a team, scale up the operation, and refine the process. They even started buying up overstock from other businesses, adding to their inventory and increasing their profits.

But the real turning point came when Ethan decided to expand beyond just his company's returns. He reached out to other warehouses, offering to help them liquidate their excess inventory in the same way. It was a win-win—he got more products to sell, and they got rid of their unwanted stock without taking a loss.

Within a year, Ethan's online store had grown into a multi-million dollar business. He was no longer just a warehouse manager—he was an entrepreneur, a problem solver, someone who had turned a frustrating situation into a life-changing opportunity. The best part? He did it by seeing value where others saw waste, by finding gold where others saw dirt.

Ethan's story is a powerful reminder that opportunity often comes disguised as a problem. It's easy to overlook, easy to dismiss, but if you're willing to dig a little deeper, you might just find something that could change your life forever. It doesn't have to be a revolutionary idea—it just has to solve a problem in a way that others haven't considered.

So, the next time you're faced with a frustrating situation, a problem that seems insurmountable, take a step back. Look at it from a different angle. Ask yourself, "Is there an opportunity here that I'm not seeing?" You might be surprised at what you find.

Remember, success isn't always about having the biggest idea or the grandest vision. Sometimes, it's about finding value in the things everyone else has overlooked. It's about turning problems into solutions, waste into profit, and frustration into fulfillment.

UNSTOPPABLE

Ethan found his path to success not by dreaming of something far off, but by looking at what was right in front of him. And if he could do it, so can you.

Keep your eyes open. Your next big opportunity might be hiding in the most unlikely place.

19

THE LEAP OF FAITH

TRUSTING YOUR GUT WHEN EVERYONE DOUBTS YOU

There's a moment in every entrepreneur's journey when you have to make a choice: play it safe or take a leap of faith into the unknown. It's the kind of decision that keeps you up at night, gnawing at you with a mix of fear and excitement. But it's also the kind of decision that can change your life forever—if you're brave enough to make it.

This is the story of Lily, who found herself standing on the edge of a cliff, looking out at a world of possibilities, with everyone around her telling her not to jump. But sometimes, you have to trust your gut, even when no one else believes in you.

Lily had always been the creative type. As a kid, she was constantly drawing, painting, and dreaming up stories that took her far away from the small town where she grew up. Her parents, practical and hardworking, encouraged her to pursue something "more stable," something that would guarantee a steady paycheck and a secure future. So, Lily did what she thought she was supposed to do—she went to college, got a degree in marketing, and landed a good job at a corporate advertising firm.

UNSTOPPABLE

For a while, it seemed like the right choice. The job was decent, the pay was good, and Lily was doing creative work—sort of. But as the years went by, she felt a growing sense of unease. The job that had once seemed full of promise started to feel more like a cage, and the creativity she loved was stifled by corporate guidelines and client demands. The spark that had once driven her was fading, and Lily couldn't shake the feeling that she was meant for something more.

Then, something happened that changed everything.

One day, while scrolling through social media, Lily came across a video that stopped her in her tracks. It was a short clip of a woman painting a mural on the side of a building. The colors were vibrant, the design was bold, and the entire process was mesmerizing. Lily felt something stir inside her—a long-forgotten dream, a passion that she had buried under years of "shoulds" and "musts."

She watched the video again, and again, until she couldn't ignore the feeling anymore. The idea started to form in her mind: what if she could do that? What if she could leave behind the corporate world and become a full-time artist, painting murals that brought color and life to the gray walls of the city?

UNSTOPPABLE

The idea was crazy. It was risky. It was completely out of left field. But the more Lily thought about it, the more she knew it was what she needed to do. She had spent too many years playing it safe, too many years doing what was expected of her. It was time to take a chance on herself, to trust her gut, and see where it led.

But not everyone saw it that way.

When Lily shared her idea with her friends and family, the reactions were less than enthusiastic. They worried about the instability, the financial risks, the uncertainty of trying to make it as an artist in a city filled with talented people. "Are you sure about this?" they asked. "What if it doesn't work out? What if you fail?"

Lily didn't have all the answers. She didn't know if it would work out, if she would make enough money to support herself, or if anyone would even want to hire her. But she knew one thing for sure—she couldn't keep living the life she was living. The thought of staying in her safe, stable job, of letting her dreams die a slow death, was more terrifying than the thought of failing.

So, she made the leap.

UNSTOPPABLE

Lily quit her job, cashed out her savings, and started from scratch. She spent her days painting, creating a portfolio of work that showcased her unique style and vision. She reached out to local businesses, offering to paint murals at a discount, just to get her foot in the door. She promoted herself online, sharing her journey on social media, and slowly but surely, the opportunities began to trickle in.

The first few months were tough. There were days when Lily questioned everything, when the bills were piling up and the work wasn't coming in fast enough. But she kept going, fueled by the passion that had been reignited inside her. She painted every day, honing her craft, pushing herself to create bigger, bolder, more ambitious pieces.

Then, one day, everything changed.

A local café owner saw Lily's work online and reached out to her. He wanted her to paint a mural on the side of his building—something that would capture the spirit of the neighborhood, something that would make people stop and take notice. Lily poured her heart into the project, creating a design that was vibrant, dynamic, and full of life. When the mural was finished, it quickly became a local sensation. People came from all over the city to see it, to take pictures in front of it, to talk about the artist who had brought it to life.

UNSTOPPABLE

That mural led to more projects, more opportunities. Lily's work was featured in local magazines, on blogs, and even in a segment on the evening news. Her murals began popping up all over the city, each one more stunning than the last. She was no longer just another artist—she was making a name for herself, building a brand, and living the life she had always dreamed of.

But it wasn't just about the success. It was about the fulfillment, the joy of doing something she loved, something that felt true to who she was. Lily had taken a leap of faith, and it had paid off in ways she never could have imagined.

Lily's story is a reminder that sometimes, you have to trust your gut, even when everyone else is telling you to play it safe. It's easy to let fear hold you back, to listen to the doubts and the "what ifs," but the truth is, the biggest risks often lead to the biggest rewards. If you have a dream, a passion that won't let go, don't be afraid to take the leap. Don't be afraid to trust yourself, even when the path ahead is uncertain.

Success doesn't come from staying in your comfort zone. It comes from stepping out into the unknown, from believing in yourself when no one else does. It comes from taking a leap of faith and trusting that you'll find your wings on the way down.

UNSTOPPABLE

Lily found her wings, and she's soaring higher than she ever thought possible. And the best part? She's doing it on her own terms, living a life that's full of color, creativity, and endless possibilities.

Your dreams are worth the risk. Your passions are worth pursuing. So take the leap, trust your gut, and see where it takes you.

Because the only thing scarier than failing is never trying at all.

20

THE UNEXPECTED MENTOR

FINDING WISDOM IN THE LEAST LIKELY PLACE

Sometimes, the guidance you need doesn't come from where you expect it. It doesn't come from a best-selling book, a TED Talk, or a seasoned professional. Sometimes, it comes from the least likely place, from someone you'd never imagine could change your life. But when you're open to it, that unexpected mentor can provide the wisdom and push you need to turn your life around.

This is the story of Jake, a guy who thought he had all the answers until he met someone who made him question everything—and in doing so, helped him find the path to his true success.

Jake was always the go-getter, the guy with the plan. In high school, he was the one everyone thought would make it big. He got a scholarship to a prestigious university, graduated with honors, and landed a job at a top consulting firm in the city. He was living in a sleek downtown apartment, wearing the latest designer suits, and climbing the corporate ladder with the kind of determination that left no room for doubt. On the outside, Jake was the picture of success.

UNSTOPPABLE

But inside, Jake was struggling. The pressure to perform, to always be the best, was wearing him down. The long hours, the constant travel, the relentless pursuit of the next big promotion—it was all taking a toll on him. But Jake wasn't the kind of guy to admit he was struggling. He pushed it all down, convincing himself that this was the price of success, that he just had to work harder, push through, and eventually, everything would fall into place.

Then came the project that nearly broke him.

Jake's firm landed a high-stakes contract with a major tech company, and Jake was put in charge. It was his big break, the opportunity to prove himself to the higher-ups and secure his place as the next rising star. But from the start, the project was a disaster. The client was demanding, the deadlines were impossible, and Jake's team was stretched to the breaking point. He was working around the clock, barely sleeping, and growing more frustrated by the day.

It all came to a head one late night when Jake's team missed a critical deadline. The client was furious, his boss was breathing down his neck, and Jake felt like he was on the verge of losing everything he'd worked for. After a particularly brutal meeting, Jake left the office and walked out into the cold night, his mind racing with thoughts of failure, fear, and desperation.

UNSTOPPABLE

As he wandered through the city, Jake found himself in a part of town he didn't usually go to—a quieter, older neighborhood that felt worlds away from the sleek, modern buildings he was used to. He walked into a small, run-down diner, the kind of place he would normally pass by without a second glance, and sat down at the counter. He wasn't even hungry—he just needed to be somewhere, anywhere, that wasn't the office.

The diner was nearly empty, except for an older man sitting a few seats down, sipping coffee and reading a newspaper. Jake didn't pay him much attention at first, too lost in his own thoughts. But after a while, the man looked over at Jake, as if sensing the turmoil inside him.

"Rough day?" the man asked, his voice calm and steady.

Jake nodded, not trusting himself to say more. The man didn't push, just sipped his coffee and turned back to his paper. But after a few moments of silence, he spoke again.

"You know, when I was your age, I thought I had to have it all figured out," he said. "Thought if I just worked hard enough, did everything right, I'd get where I wanted to go. But life has a way of showing you that it doesn't always work out the way you plan."

UNSTOPPABLE

Jake glanced over at the man, surprised by the words. He looked like someone who had seen a lot in his life—gray hair, weathered face, the kind of lines around his eyes that come from both laughter and tears. There was something about him that felt genuine, grounded, like he knew things that couldn't be learned from books or business school.

"What do you do?" Jake found himself asking, curious despite himself.

The man smiled, a little sadly. "Used to be a lot like you, I think. Chased after success, climbed the ladder, did everything I thought I was supposed to do. But then... well, let's just say life had other plans."

Jake didn't know why, but he found himself opening up to this stranger, telling him about the project, the pressure, the fear that he was losing control of everything he'd built. The man listened quietly, nodding occasionally, but not interrupting. When Jake finished, the man set down his coffee and looked him in the eye.

"Here's the thing, kid," he said. "Success isn't about how much you can do or how fast you can do it. It's about understanding what really matters to you. I spent years chasing something that I thought was success, but it was just a mirage. It wasn't until I lost it all that I realized what I really wanted. And by then, it was too late."

UNSTOPPABLE

Jake felt a knot tighten in his chest. "What did you do?"

The man shrugged. "Started over. Found work that made me happy, not just rich. It wasn't easy, but it was worth it. I learned that sometimes, you have to lose what you think you want to find what you really need."

Jake sat there, letting the words sink in. He knew the man was right. He had been so focused on achieving, on winning, that he hadn't stopped to think about whether the life he was building was the one he really wanted. The idea of losing everything terrified him, but the thought of continuing on this path, of burning out and ending up with nothing, scared him even more.

The next morning, Jake made a decision. He walked into his boss's office and asked for a meeting. It wasn't easy, and his boss wasn't thrilled, but Jake explained that he needed to take a step back, to reassess his role, his goals, and how he wanted to move forward. It was a risk—he knew it could cost him the promotion, maybe even his job—but for the first time in a long time, Jake felt like he was in control.

UNSTOPPABLE

Over the next few weeks, Jake began to redefine his approach to work. He delegated more, focused on the tasks that truly mattered, and made time for the things that brought him joy outside of work. It wasn't about working less—it was about working smarter, about finding a balance that allowed him to be successful without losing himself in the process.

And the most surprising thing? His work got better. The project that had nearly broken him started to turn around. His team responded to his new leadership style, and they began to meet their deadlines with renewed energy. The client, who had been on the verge of pulling the contract, started to come back on board. Jake's boss noticed the change, too—he saw that Jake wasn't just a hard worker, but a smart one, someone who could see the bigger picture.

In the end, Jake got that promotion. But more importantly, he found a way to succeed on his own terms. He didn't just climb the ladder—he built his own path, one that allowed him to grow, to thrive, and to enjoy the journey as much as the destination.

Jake never saw the man from the diner again, but he thought about him often. He realized that sometimes, the wisdom you need comes from the most unexpected places, from people who have walked the path before you and learned the hard lessons. And if you're open to it, that wisdom can change everything.

So, if you find yourself lost, overwhelmed, or questioning the path you're on, don't be afraid to look for guidance in unexpected places. Listen to the voices that come from outside your usual circle, from those who see things differently. You never know where the advice you need might come from—or how it might help you find your way.

Success isn't just about the destination. It's about the journey, the choices you make, and the lessons you learn along the way. And sometimes, the best lessons come from the most unlikely teachers.

Keep your eyes and ears open. Your next breakthrough might be just a conversation away.

21  THE SILENT STRUGGLE

FINDING STRENGTH IN THE SHADOWS

Everyone has a story, but not everyone's story is told. Sometimes, the most profound battles happen in silence, away from the spotlight, where the world can't see. It's in these moments, when the world isn't watching, that true strength is forged. This is the story of Sarah, who faced her darkest hours in silence, only to emerge stronger, wiser, and on the path to a success she never imagined.

Sarah was the kind of person everyone admired. She was smart, driven, and always had a smile on her face. In college, she was the one everyone turned to for help, the one who seemed to have it all together. After graduation, she landed a job at a prestigious law firm, a dream come true for someone who had worked so hard to get there. She was on track to become a top attorney, and her future looked bright.

But behind the smile, Sarah was struggling. The pressure of the job was immense—the long hours, the demanding clients, the constant need to prove herself. She was drowning in work, barely sleeping, and the stress was beginning to take a toll. But Sarah didn't let anyone see it. She kept up the façade, convinced that if she just pushed a little harder, things would get better.

They didn't.

UNSTOPPABLE

The breaking point came one winter evening. Sarah was in the office, long after everyone else had gone home. She was working on a case that had been consuming her for weeks—barely eating, barely sleeping, barely living outside of work. The phone rang, and when she answered, it was her mother, calling to check in.

"Sarah, you sound tired," her mother said gently. "Are you taking care of yourself?"

That simple question hit Sarah like a ton of bricks. She realized in that moment just how far she had fallen, how she had been neglecting not just her health, but her happiness, her well-being, her life. She felt the tears well up, but she swallowed them back, determined to stay strong, to keep up the act.

"I'm fine, Mom," she lied. "Just a lot going on at work."

After she hung up, Sarah sat in the darkened office, staring at the piles of paperwork in front of her. The weight of everything she had been holding in came crashing down, and for the first time, she allowed herself to feel it. The exhaustion, the fear, the overwhelming sense that she was losing herself in a life that was supposed to be her dream.

UNSTOPPABLE

She knew something had to change, but she didn't know how. The next few weeks were a blur of anxiety and sleepless nights. She was caught in a vicious cycle—too overwhelmed to see a way out, too scared to ask for help. The pressure built until she couldn't take it anymore.

One night, after another 14-hour day, Sarah found herself standing on the balcony of her apartment, looking out at the city lights. She felt utterly alone, despite being surrounded by millions of people. The loneliness, the pressure, the fear—it was all too much. She had never felt so close to giving up.

But then, something inside her snapped. A voice, quiet but firm, rose up from deep within.

"This is not the end. You are stronger than this."

It was like a light breaking through the darkness. Sarah realized that she had been so focused on maintaining the image of success that she had forgotten what success really meant to her. It wasn't about climbing the corporate ladder at all costs, about sacrificing her health and happiness for a career that was killing her. It was about finding balance, about living a life that made her feel alive, not just accomplished.

UNSTOPPABLE

Sarah made a decision that night. She wasn't going to let this job, this pressure, this fear define her. She was going to take control of her life, even if it meant stepping back from the path she had worked so hard to follow.

The next morning, she walked into her boss's office and did something she never thought she'd have the courage to do—she asked for help. She explained that she was struggling, that the workload was too much, that she needed to find a way to balance her job with her life. It wasn't easy to admit, and she feared the consequences, but she knew it was the right thing to do.

To her surprise, her boss didn't criticize or judge her. Instead, he listened. He acknowledged the pressure that everyone was under and agreed to lighten her load, to give her the space she needed to find her footing again. It was the first step in a long journey back to herself.

Over the next few months, Sarah began to rebuild her life. She started setting boundaries at work, leaving the office at a reasonable hour, and prioritizing her health. She took up yoga, started journaling, and reconnected with friends she had pushed away during her darkest days. She realized that success wasn't about burning herself out—it was about finding a way to thrive in all aspects of her life.

UNSTOPPABLE

And then, something unexpected happened. As Sarah focused on her well-being, her work improved. She became more efficient, more creative, more confident in her abilities. Her clients noticed the change, and so did her colleagues. She wasn't just surviving—she was excelling, but this time, on her own terms.

But the most important change was inside her. Sarah found a strength she didn't know she had—a resilience forged in the silence of her struggle. She learned that asking for help wasn't a sign of weakness, but of courage. She discovered that true success isn't about how much you can handle, but about how well you can balance the challenges life throws at you.

Sarah's story is a reminder that the journey to success isn't always visible to the outside world. Sometimes, the hardest battles are fought in silence, in the quiet moments when no one is watching. But those battles are where true strength is born, where the foundation for real success is laid.

If you're struggling in silence, if you're facing your own dark night and wondering how you'll make it through, remember Sarah's story. Remember that you are not alone, and that asking for help is a step forward, not a step back. It's okay to be vulnerable, to admit that you can't do it all on your own. Because in that vulnerability, you find your strength.

UNSTOPPABLE

Success isn't about never falling. It's about getting back up, every time, stronger and more determined than before. It's about finding balance, about knowing when to push forward and when to pull back. And it's about recognizing that your worth isn't defined by your work, but by the life you build for yourself.

So, if you're in the shadows right now, know that there is light on the other side. You have the strength to make it through, to rise above the challenges, and to create a life that truly fulfills you. Take it one step at a time, trust in your resilience, and know that you are stronger than you think.

Because the real story of success isn't written in the easy moments —it's written in the struggle, in the perseverance, and in the quiet courage to keep going, even when the world doesn't see.

Your story is still being written. Make it one worth telling.

22 — THE UNEXPECTED TURN

WHEN LIFE FORCES YOU TO RETHINK EVERYTHING

Life has a way of throwing curveballs when you least expect them, pushing you to the edge and forcing you to rethink everything you thought you knew. It's in those moments, when the future feels uncertain and the ground beneath you is shaky, that you find out who you really are. This is the story of Matt, a man whose life took an unexpected turn, leading him down a path he never imagined, but one that ultimately changed his life forever.

Matt had always been the steady one—the guy who played by the rules, who did everything right. He went to a good college, got a degree in business, and landed a stable job at a reputable company. He wasn't chasing after fame or fortune; he just wanted a comfortable life, something predictable and secure. And for a while, that's exactly what he had.

Matt's life was a picture of stability. He had a good job, a modest house in a quiet neighborhood, and a circle of friends he could count on. He wasn't the kind of person who took risks or ventured outside of his comfort zone. He liked things to be orderly, controlled, and safe.

But all of that changed in an instant.

UNSTOPPABLE

It was a rainy Tuesday morning when Matt's phone rang. He was getting ready for work, sipping his usual cup of black coffee, when he saw his boss's name on the screen. He answered, expecting the usual work talk, but the voice on the other end was different—somber, serious.

"Matt, I'm sorry to have to tell you this, but the company is downsizing. Your position is being eliminated."

The words hit Matt like a punch to the gut. He felt the room spin around him, the ground beneath his feet giving way. This couldn't be happening. He had done everything right, followed all the rules. How could this be happening to him?

In the days that followed, Matt felt like he was living in a nightmare. He went through the motions—packing up his desk, signing paperwork, saying goodbye to colleagues—but inside, he was in free fall. The life he had built so carefully, so methodically, was crumbling, and he didn't know how to stop it.

For the first time in his life, Matt was facing an uncertain future. The safety net he had relied on was gone, and he was left with nothing but questions. What would he do now? How would he pay the bills? Who was he without the job that had defined him for so long?

UNSTOPPABLE

The weeks turned into months, and despite his best efforts, Matt couldn't find another job. The economy was tough, the competition was fierce, and he was beginning to feel like he was drowning. The savings he had carefully built up were dwindling, and the pressure was mounting. He felt lost, adrift, with no clear direction and no idea how to move forward.

One night, after another fruitless day of job searching, Matt found himself sitting on his porch, staring out into the darkness. The weight of everything he had been holding in—the fear, the frustration, the hopelessness—was crushing him. He felt like he was at the end of his rope, like there was no way out.

But then, a thought crossed his mind, something he hadn't allowed himself to consider before. What if this wasn't the end? What if this unexpected turn, this loss, was actually an opportunity in disguise? The idea was terrifying, but it was also liberating. For the first time, Matt realized that he wasn't tied to the life he had lost. He was free to create something new.

Matt decided to take a chance on something he had always been passionate about but had never pursued—woodworking. It was a hobby he had picked up in his early twenties, something he loved but had always seen as just that—a hobby. But now, with nothing to lose, he wondered if it could be more.

UNSTOPPABLE

He started small, using the tools he already had and the garage as his workshop. He began crafting furniture—simple pieces at first, but with time, his skills improved. The process of creating something with his own hands, of turning raw materials into something beautiful and functional, brought him a sense of peace he hadn't felt in months.

Matt wasn't sure if anyone would buy his furniture, but he decided to give it a shot. He set up a small online store, took some photos of his work, and put it out there. He didn't have high expectations—he just wanted to see what would happen.

And then, to his surprise, the orders started coming in.

At first, it was just a few pieces here and there—a coffee table, a bookshelf—but as word spread, his business began to grow. People loved the craftsmanship, the attention to detail, the fact that every piece was handmade with care. Matt found himself working long hours in his garage, not because he had to, but because he wanted to. For the first time in a long time, he felt a sense of purpose, of fulfillment.

As his business grew, Matt realized that this unexpected turn had given him something he hadn't even known he was missing—a chance to do something he was truly passionate about. He wasn't just making furniture; he was building a new life, one that was richer, more fulfilling, and more meaningful than the one he had lost.

UNSTOPPABLE

The money started coming in, too. Slowly at first, but then more steadily. Within a year, Matt was making more from his woodworking business than he had in his old corporate job. But more importantly, he was happy. He had found a way to turn a painful loss into a new beginning, to create something beautiful out of the chaos.

Matt's story is a reminder that sometimes, life's most painful moments are the ones that open the door to something new, something better. It's easy to get stuck in a life that feels safe, to cling to the familiar even when it's no longer serving you. But when life forces you to let go, when it pushes you into the unknown, that's when you have the opportunity to discover who you really are.

If you're facing an unexpected turn, if life has thrown you a curveball and you're not sure how to handle it, remember Matt's story. Remember that the end of one chapter is just the beginning of another, and that you have the power to write the next part of your story. It won't be easy, and it won't happen overnight, but if you're willing to take a chance, to trust yourself, and to embrace the uncertainty, you might just find that your greatest success is waiting on the other side.

Life doesn't always go according to plan. But sometimes, the best things happen when you're forced to step off the path you thought you were supposed to follow.

UNSTOPPABLE

So take a deep breath, trust the journey, and see where the unexpected turn takes you. Because the road less traveled might just lead you to exactly where you're meant to be.

UNSTOPPABLE

THE RISK THAT PAID OFF

BETTING ON YOURSELF WHEN THE ODDS ARE AGAINST YOU

In every success story, there's a moment when everything is on the line—a moment where you have to decide whether to play it safe or take a risk that could change your life forever. It's terrifying, exhilarating, and often, it's the defining moment that separates those who dream from those who achieve. This is the story of Mia, who took a gamble on herself when the odds were stacked against her and ended up winning in ways she never expected.

Mia had always been a dreamer. Growing up in a small town, she spent most of her time with her nose in a book or sketching designs for clothes she imagined someday creating. But dreams don't pay the bills, and by the time she graduated high school, the pressure to be practical weighed heavy on her. So, like so many others, she put her dreams on hold and enrolled in a nearby community college, studying business—a "safe" choice, according to her parents.

For a few years, Mia went through the motions. She got decent grades, worked part-time jobs, and did what she was supposed to do. But that spark, the one that had lit up her world when she was a child, had dimmed. She couldn't shake the feeling that she was letting her life slip away, trading her passion for a security that didn't even feel real.

UNSTOPPABLE

After college, Mia landed a steady job as an administrative assistant at a local insurance company. It wasn't glamorous, but it was stable, and stability was what everyone around her valued. She worked hard, saved her money, and tried to convince herself that this was enough.

But it wasn't. Not for Mia.

Every day, as she sat behind her desk, answering phones and filing paperwork, she couldn't stop thinking about the life she wanted—the life she had dreamed of as a child. The life where she wasn't just pushing papers, but creating something, building something, living with passion and purpose. The thought gnawed at her, day after day, until she couldn't ignore it anymore.

One evening, after another mind-numbing day at the office, Mia found herself in front of her old sewing machine. It had been years since she'd used it, but something pulled her toward it that night. She dusted it off, pulled out some fabric scraps, and started to sew. The rhythm of the needle, the feel of the fabric, the act of creating something from nothing—it brought her a sense of peace and excitement she hadn't felt in years.

That night, Mia made a decision. She was going to bet on herself. She was going to take the risk she had been too scared to take for so long. She was going to start her own clothing line.

UNSTOPPABLE

The idea seemed crazy. She had no formal training in fashion design, no experience in running a business, and barely enough money in her savings to cover her rent, let alone fund a startup. But the thought of continuing on the path she was on, of living a life that wasn't truly hers, was even scarier.

Mia started small. She spent her evenings and weekends designing clothes, sewing samples, and researching everything she could about the fashion industry. She watched countless YouTube tutorials, read books, and reached out to people in the industry for advice. It was overwhelming, exhausting, and at times, downright terrifying. But for the first time in a long time, she felt alive.

After months of hard work, Mia finally had her first collection ready. It wasn't much—just a few pieces she had made herself—but it was hers. She created a simple website, took some photos of the clothes, and put them up for sale. She didn't know what to expect, but she knew she had to try.

The first few weeks were rough. The sales trickled in, but they were far from enough to sustain her. She was running out of money, her credit cards were maxed out, and the doubt was creeping in. Had she made a huge mistake? Was this just another failed dream?

UNSTOPPABLE

But then, something incredible happened. One of her pieces—a simple, elegant dress—caught the eye of a popular fashion blogger. The blogger featured it in a post, raving about the quality and unique design. The post went viral, and within days, Mia's website was flooded with orders. She was selling out faster than she could keep up, and suddenly, the dream that had once seemed so out of reach was within her grasp.

The success was exhilarating, but it was also overwhelming. Mia had to scale up quickly—hiring seamstresses, finding a manufacturer, and managing the growing demands of her business. She made mistakes, faced setbacks, and had more sleepless nights than she could count. But she kept going, driven by the belief that this was what she was meant to do.

Within a year, Mia's clothing line had become a full-fledged business, with her pieces being sold in boutiques across the country and featured in fashion magazines. She had gone from being an administrative assistant in a small town to a successful entrepreneur, living her dream and building something she was truly proud of.

But the real victory wasn't just in the success—it was in the journey. Mia had taken a risk, bet on herself when the odds were against her, and proved that she could make her dreams a reality. She had faced her fears, pushed through the doubt, and discovered a strength and resilience she didn't know she had.

UNSTOPPABLE

Mia's story is a powerful reminder that sometimes, the biggest rewards come from the biggest risks. It's easy to stay in your comfort zone, to choose the safe path, but real success, the kind that fills your soul, often requires you to step out into the unknown, to take a chance on yourself, even when everyone else thinks you're crazy.

If you're standing at a crossroads, if you're facing a decision that could change your life, remember Mia's story. Remember that the fear you feel is normal, but it doesn't have to hold you back. The path to success isn't always clear, and it's rarely easy, but if you're willing to take the risk, to bet on yourself, you might just find that the life you've been dreaming of is waiting for you on the other side.

Don't let fear keep you from living the life you want. Don't let doubt stop you from chasing your dreams. Take the risk, trust yourself, and see where it takes you.

Because the greatest success stories aren't about playing it safe—they're about daring to take the leap, even when the odds are against you.

THE BREAKING POINT

WHEN EVERYTHING FALLS APART BEFORE IT COMES TOGETHER

Sometimes, you have to hit rock bottom before you can rise to the top. It's in the moments of deepest despair, when everything seems lost, that the seeds of greatness are often planted. This is the story of Josh, a man who thought he had lost it all, only to discover that hitting rock bottom was the beginning of his climb to the top.

Josh was the kind of guy everyone expected to succeed. In high school, he was the star quarterback, the golden boy with a bright future. He got a full scholarship to a prestigious university, where he excelled both on the field and in the classroom. By the time he graduated, he had job offers lined up and a clear path ahead of him. It seemed like nothing could go wrong.

But life had other plans.

After college, Josh took a high-paying job at a major tech company, a position that everyone envied. At first, things were great—he was making good money, living in a fancy apartment, and climbing the corporate ladder. But as the years went by, the pressure started to build. The job that had once seemed exciting turned into a grind. The long hours, the constant demands, the cutthroat competition—it was all starting to wear him down.

UNSTOPPABLE

Josh tried to keep up the façade, to act like everything was fine. He worked harder, stayed later, and pushed himself to the brink. But inside, he was struggling. The stress was eating away at him, and the things he once loved—his hobbies, his relationships, even his job—began to feel like burdens. He was burning out, but he didn't know how to stop.

Then, one day, it all came crashing down.

It started with a mistake—a small one, something that wouldn't have mattered if things had been different. But in the high-stakes world of corporate tech, there was no room for error. The mistake led to a missed deadline, which led to a botched project, which led to a very public reprimand from his boss. Josh was humiliated, his confidence shattered.

But that was just the beginning.

Over the next few months, things went from bad to worse. The stress took its toll on Josh's health, and he started missing work, falling behind, and making more mistakes. His boss lost faith in him, his colleagues distanced themselves, and soon, the job he had once been so proud of became a daily nightmare. The final blow came when he was called into his boss's office and told that his position was being eliminated.

Just like that, it was over.

UNSTOPPABLE

Josh walked out of the office with a box of his belongings and a sense of total defeat. The life he had worked so hard to build was crumbling around him, and he didn't know what to do. He had lost his job, his purpose, and his identity all at once. The future that had once seemed so bright now felt like a dark, empty void.

For weeks, Josh spiraled. He spent his days lying on the couch, staring at the ceiling, and wondering how everything had gone so wrong. He stopped answering his phone, stopped talking to his friends, and stopped caring about anything. The man who had once been so full of energy, so driven and ambitious, was now a shadow of his former self.

But then, something changed.

One night, as Josh sat alone in his apartment, surrounded by the silence of his own thoughts, he realized that he had two choices: he could let this defeat define him, or he could find a way to rise above it. He knew he couldn't go back to the life he had lost, but maybe, just maybe, he could build something new.

Josh decided to take the first step.

UNSTOPPABLE

He started small, forcing himself to get out of bed each morning, to go for a run, to do something—anything—that made him feel alive again. He began to reconnect with old friends, to talk about what had happened, to admit that he was struggling. It wasn't easy, and there were days when he felt like giving up, but slowly, he began to see a glimmer of hope.

As he started to regain his strength, Josh began to think about what he really wanted out of life. The corporate world, with all its pressures and demands, no longer held any appeal for him. He wanted to do something that mattered, something that made a difference—not just for himself, but for others. He wanted to build something that he could be proud of, something that reflected who he really was.

That's when the idea came to him.

Josh had always been passionate about fitness, ever since his days as a quarterback. It was the one thing that had kept him grounded during his darkest moments, the one thing that had given him a sense of purpose when everything else had fallen apart. He started to wonder if he could turn that passion into a business—something that would help others find the same strength and resilience that had saved him.

With nothing left to lose, Josh threw himself into the idea. He started by getting certified as a personal trainer, learning everything he could about fitness, nutrition, and wellness. He began training friends and acquaintances, building a small client base, and refining his approach. The more he worked, the more he realized that this was what he was meant to do—not sit behind a desk, but help people transform their lives.

Josh's business grew slowly at first, but word spread quickly. People were drawn to his story, to his passion, and to the genuine care he showed for each of his clients. He wasn't just helping people get in shape—he was helping them rebuild their lives, just as he had rebuilt his own.

Within a year, Josh had opened his own fitness studio, a place where people from all walks of life could come to find strength, both physical and mental. The studio became a community, a place of healing and transformation, and Josh found a sense of fulfillment he had never known before. He wasn't just successful—he was truly happy, living a life that was rich in purpose and meaning.

Josh's story is a testament to the power of resilience, to the idea that sometimes, you have to lose everything to find out what really matters. It's easy to get caught up in the race for success, to measure your worth by your job title or your bank account, but real success isn't about what you have—it's about who you are.

UNSTOPPABLE

If you're facing your own breaking point, if you're standing in the ruins of a life that you thought was unbreakable, remember Josh's story. Remember that hitting rock bottom isn't the end—it's the beginning of something new, something better. It's an opportunity to rebuild, to redefine yourself, and to create a life that is truly yours.

Don't be afraid to start over. Don't be afraid to take the lessons you've learned from your failures and use them to build something great. The path to success is rarely straight, and it's often paved with setbacks and challenges. But if you're willing to keep going, to keep pushing through the darkness, you'll find that the light on the other side is brighter than you ever imagined.

So take a deep breath, stand up, and start again. The best part of your story is still waiting to be written.

25 THE DARK BEFORE THE DAWN

TURNING DESPERATION INTO DESTINY

Every story of success has a chapter that seems impossible to get through—a time when the world feels like it's closing in, when every option seems like a dead end, and when hope is nothing more than a flicker in the dark. It's in these moments of despair that the seeds of greatness are often sown, even if you can't see it yet. This is the story of Emily, a woman who found herself on the edge of a cliff, only to discover that her greatest leap came from the darkest moment in her life.

Emily was the type of person who always had it together. She was organized, disciplined, and determined to succeed. Growing up, she was the overachiever, the straight-A student, the one who everyone knew would go on to do big things. She worked her way through college, earning a degree in graphic design, and quickly landed a job at a well-known marketing agency in the city. For a while, everything was going according to plan.

But life doesn't always follow the plan.

Emily's job started out as a dream come true. She loved the creativity, the fast-paced environment, and the thrill of working with big clients. But as time went on, the pressures of the job began to mount. The deadlines were relentless, the competition fierce, and the demands never-ending. Emily started working longer hours, sacrificing her personal life, and pushing herself to the limit to meet the expectations of her bosses and clients.

UNSTOPPABLE

The burnout crept up slowly, like a shadow that grew darker and darker with each passing day. Emily began to dread going to work, her passion for design fading into a sense of obligation and exhaustion. The spark that had once driven her was gone, replaced by a constant feeling of anxiety and a growing sense of despair.

Then, in the middle of a particularly brutal project, Emily's world came crashing down.

One morning, as she was rushing to get to the office, Emily received a phone call that would change everything. Her mother, who had been battling a long illness, had taken a turn for the worse. The doctors didn't know how much time she had left. Emily's heart shattered. She left work immediately, heading back to her hometown to be with her family.

Over the next few weeks, Emily's life was a blur of hospital visits, sleepless nights, and emotional turmoil. She tried to balance work with being there for her mother, but it was impossible. The stress was overwhelming, and the thought of losing her mom was more than she could bear. Eventually, something had to give. Her work started to suffer, and soon, her boss called her in for a meeting.

"We're going to have to let you go," he said, his voice heavy with regret. "We know you're dealing with a lot, but we need someone who can give 100% right now."

UNSTOPPABLE

Just like that, Emily lost her job. In the span of a few weeks, her entire life had fallen apart—her career, her stability, and now, her mother. She felt like she was drowning, unable to catch her breath as the waves of grief and fear crashed over her.

The weeks that followed were the darkest of Emily's life. She moved back in with her parents to care for her mother full-time, putting her career on hold indefinitely. She felt completely lost, like everything she had worked for was slipping through her fingers. The future she had envisioned for herself was gone, and she didn't know how to move forward.

But in the midst of her darkest hour, something unexpected happened.

One afternoon, as she sat by her mother's bedside, Emily picked up a sketchbook that had been lying on the table. It was something she hadn't touched in months, maybe years. She began to draw—simple sketches at first, just to pass the time. But as the days went by, the drawings became more intricate, more expressive. The act of creating, of pouring her emotions onto the page, became a lifeline, a way to process the pain she was feeling.

UNSTOPPABLE

Emily started to post her drawings on social media, not thinking much of it. She didn't expect anyone to notice—she was doing it for herself, a way to cope with the grief that was consuming her. But people did notice. Her friends, then friends of friends, and soon, strangers from all over were commenting on her work, sharing it, and telling her how much her art resonated with them.

The response was overwhelming, and for the first time in months, Emily felt a glimmer of hope. Her art, born out of the darkest time in her life, was touching people in a way she had never imagined. It gave her a sense of purpose, a reason to keep going, even when everything else felt hopeless.

As her following grew, so did the opportunities. A local art gallery reached out, offering to showcase her work in an exhibition. Then a well-known online platform asked her to collaborate on a series of illustrations. Before she knew it, Emily was being commissioned for projects, her art featured in publications, and her name starting to spread in the art community.

What started as a way to cope with pain turned into a career she never saw coming. Emily wasn't just surviving—she was thriving, using her talent and passion to create something beautiful out of the ashes of her old life. She had found a new path, one that allowed her to express herself, to connect with others, and to build a life that was richer and more meaningful than the one she had lost.

UNSTOPPABLE

Emily's mother passed away peacefully, knowing that her daughter had found her way. Emily continued to honor her mother's memory through her art, creating pieces that celebrated life, love, and the resilience of the human spirit. Her work became known for its emotional depth, its raw honesty, and its ability to touch the hearts of those who saw it.

Emily's story is a testament to the power of creativity, to the idea that even in the darkest of times, there is light to be found. It's a reminder that sometimes, the things that break us also have the power to make us whole again. It's about finding strength in vulnerability, about using pain as a catalyst for growth, and about discovering that when life takes everything from you, it also gives you the chance to rebuild.

If you're in a dark place right now, if you're struggling to see a way forward, remember Emily's story. Remember that the darkness doesn't last forever, and that sometimes, it's in the depths of despair that we find our true purpose. It's okay to feel lost, to grieve, to be afraid—but don't give up. Keep going, keep creating, keep searching for that flicker of light.

Because the dawn always comes after the darkest hour. And when it does, it brings with it the chance to start again, to create something new, and to live a life that's more beautiful than you ever imagined.

UNSTOPPABLE

Your darkest moment could be the beginning of your greatest triumph. Don't be afraid to find out.

26

THE SILENT SACRIFICE

WHEN YOU GIVE EVERYTHING AND STILL COME UP SHORT

There's a special kind of pain in giving everything you've got—your time, your energy, your heart—and still falling short. It's the kind of pain that makes you question everything, makes you wonder if you're wasting your life chasing a dream that's never going to come true. But sometimes, it's the very act of pushing through that pain, of refusing to give up, that leads to a breakthrough you never saw coming. This is the story of Lisa, a woman who gave it all, lost almost everything, and found out that sometimes, the reward comes not in spite of the struggle, but because of it.

Lisa had always been a fighter. Growing up in a tough neighborhood, she learned early on that nothing was going to be handed to her. If she wanted something, she had to work for it, and work she did. She put herself through college, juggling multiple jobs and a full course load, determined to make something of herself. And she did—graduating with honors and landing a good job at a promising startup.

For the first time, it felt like all the sacrifices had been worth it. Lisa threw herself into her work, driven by the same fire that had gotten her through college. She worked late into the night, often being the last to leave the office. She sacrificed weekends, relationships, and even her health, all in the name of building something that mattered. She believed in the startup's mission, believed that her hard work would pay off, and believed that she was on the path to something great.

UNSTOPPABLE

But belief doesn't always align with reality.

After years of grinding away, Lisa started to notice the cracks in the foundation. The startup that had once been full of promise was struggling—clients were pulling out, investors were losing faith, and the team that had once been so tight-knit was starting to fracture. The long hours and relentless pressure were taking a toll on everyone, but especially on Lisa. She was exhausted, burned out, and starting to question if all the sacrifices she'd made were worth it.

Then came the day that shattered everything.

The company's biggest investor pulled out at the last minute, leaving the startup teetering on the edge of bankruptcy. Without that funding, there was no way to keep the lights on, no way to pay the employees who had given everything to make the company succeed. The founder called an emergency meeting, and with a heavy heart, announced that the company was shutting down.

Just like that, it was over.

Lisa sat in the conference room, surrounded by her colleagues—her friends—staring blankly at the table in front of her. It felt like the ground had been pulled out from under her. All those late nights, all those missed birthdays, all the times she'd chosen work over life—it all seemed like a waste. She had given everything, and it still wasn't enough.

UNSTOPPABLE

The next few weeks were a blur of sadness and confusion. Lisa found herself back in her small apartment, the walls closing in around her. She was unemployed, broke, and completely drained. She felt like she had nothing left to give, like all the fight had been beaten out of her. The dream she had been chasing for so long had turned into a nightmare, and she didn't know how to move forward.

But then, something unexpected happened.

One evening, as she was scrolling through job listings, feeling more hopeless by the minute, Lisa got a call from an old friend—a woman she hadn't spoken to in years. They had met in college, bonded over their shared drive to succeed, and had kept in touch sporadically over the years. The friend had heard about the company's collapse and wanted to check in.

"I'm so sorry to hear what happened," she said. "But you know, Lisa, I've always admired your resilience. You've got something special—a way of seeing things that other people don't. Have you ever thought about starting your own business?"

Lisa almost laughed at the suggestion. Start her own business? After everything that had just happened? The thought seemed ridiculous. She had just watched a company she believed in fall apart despite all her hard work. How could she possibly think about starting something new?

UNSTOPPABLE

But the idea wouldn't leave her alone. Over the next few days, it kept popping up in her mind, refusing to be ignored. She started thinking about all the things she had learned during her time at the startup—all the mistakes that had been made, all the things she would do differently if she had the chance. And slowly, a plan began to form.

Lisa decided to take the risk. She had nothing left to lose, and the idea of doing something on her own terms, of taking everything she had learned and using it to build something better, started to feel like the only way forward. She spent weeks crafting a business plan, pulling together what little savings she had left, and reaching out to potential partners and investors.

It wasn't easy. Every step of the way, Lisa was haunted by doubts and fears, memories of the failure that had nearly broken her. But she kept going, driven by a newfound sense of purpose, by the realization that her previous sacrifices hadn't been in vain. They had been preparing her for this moment, for the chance to build something stronger, something that was truly hers.

Months passed, and slowly but surely, Lisa's business started to take shape. She launched a small consulting firm, helping other startups avoid the pitfalls that had brought down the company she had worked for. Her approach was practical, no-nonsense, and deeply informed by the lessons she had learned the hard way. Clients began to take notice, and word spread about the woman who had turned her greatest failure into a new beginning.

UNSTOPPABLE

Within a year, Lisa's firm was thriving. She had built a team, expanded her services, and was making more money than she ever had before. But more importantly, she had found a sense of fulfillment that she had never known in her previous job. She wasn't just working for a paycheck—she was building something meaningful, something that made a difference.

Lisa's story is a powerful reminder that success isn't always about winning; sometimes, it's about getting back up after you've been knocked down. It's about realizing that the sacrifices you make along the way, even the ones that seem like they were for nothing, are actually the building blocks of something greater. It's about understanding that failure isn't the end—it's just a detour on the road to something better.

If you're in a place right now where it feels like everything you've worked for is slipping away, where the sacrifices you've made seem pointless, remember Lisa's story. Remember that the darkest moments often come right before the breakthrough, and that sometimes, the only way to get to where you're meant to be is to push through the pain.

Don't give up. Don't let the setbacks define you. Use them. Learn from them. Let them make you stronger, smarter, and more determined than ever before.

UNSTOPPABLE

Because the truth is, the road to success is rarely a straight line. It's full of twists and turns, ups and downs, and moments when you're not sure you can keep going. But if you do—if you keep moving forward, keep believing in yourself—you'll find that the sacrifices you made weren't in vain. They were the foundation of something far greater than you ever imagined.

Your breakthrough is closer than you think. Keep going. Keep fighting. And when you come out on the other side, you'll see that every step, every sacrifice, was worth it.

THE COST OF SUCCESS

WHEN WINNING ALMOST TAKES EVERYTHING

Success can be a double-edged sword. Sometimes, the very thing you've been striving for, dreaming about, and working toward comes at a cost so high you wonder if it was worth it at all. This is the story of Alex, a man who reached the top, only to realize that the climb had nearly destroyed everything he held dear. It's a story about the thin line between ambition and obsession, and the painful realization that winning isn't everything if you lose yourself along the way.

Alex was always driven. Growing up in a small town, he was the kid who refused to settle for mediocrity. He wanted more—more than the simple life his parents lived, more than the ordinary future everyone expected him to have. He was smart, hardworking, and fiercely ambitious. He believed that with enough determination, he could achieve anything.

After college, Alex moved to the city with big dreams and even bigger plans. He started his own tech company, pouring every ounce of energy into making it a success. He worked day and night, often sleeping at the office, fueled by the belief that all the sacrifices would pay off in the end. And they did—at first.

UNSTOPPABLE

The company took off. Alex's innovative ideas caught the attention of investors, and before long, he was leading a team of brilliant minds, building products that were changing the industry. The money started rolling in, and with it came the recognition and respect he had always craved. He was featured in magazines, invited to speak at conferences, and hailed as one of the brightest young entrepreneurs in the country.

But with success came pressure, and with pressure came the relentless drive to keep pushing, keep growing, keep winning. Alex was never satisfied. No matter how much his company achieved, it was never enough. There was always another milestone to reach, another competitor to outpace, another mountain to climb. He became obsessed with growth, with scaling the business to heights no one had ever imagined.

As the company grew, so did Alex's workload. He was constantly on the move—traveling to meetings, negotiating deals, overseeing every aspect of the business. The demands were endless, and the pressure was suffocating. But Alex couldn't stop. He was addicted to the thrill of success, to the adrenaline rush that came with every new victory.

But while Alex was winning in business, he was losing in life.

UNSTOPPABLE

His marriage, once a source of strength and comfort, began to crumble under the weight of his absence. His wife, Emily, had been supportive of his dreams from the start, but as the years went by, she felt more and more like a stranger in her own home. Alex was never there—physically or emotionally. He missed anniversaries, birthdays, even the birth of their first child, all because there was always something more important, something that couldn't wait.

Emily tried to talk to him, to make him see what was happening, but Alex was too caught up in his world to listen. He convinced himself that it was all for them—that once he achieved his goals, they could enjoy the rewards together. But deep down, he knew he was lying to himself. He was chasing something that could never be caught, and in the process, he was losing the people who mattered most.

Then came the day that brought everything crashing down.

It was a Friday evening, and Alex was in the middle of negotiating a major deal—one that would take the company to the next level. He was in his office, surrounded by papers, pacing the floor as he talked on the phone, when Emily walked in. She stood in the doorway, holding their daughter in her arms, her eyes filled with sadness.

"We need to talk, Alex," she said quietly.

UNSTOPPABLE

But Alex barely looked up. "Not now, Em. I'm in the middle of something big."

Emily's voice trembled as she spoke. "This can't wait."

Alex finally looked at her, frustration and exhaustion written all over his face. "What is it, then?"

Emily took a deep breath. "I'm leaving, Alex. I'm taking Lily, and we're leaving."

For a moment, Alex thought he hadn't heard her right. "What? You're leaving? Why? Where are you going?"

Tears welled up in Emily's eyes. "I can't do this anymore, Alex. I love you, but you're not here. You're never here. And I can't keep pretending that this is a life we can live."

Alex felt like the ground was crumbling beneath him. "Emily, please, let's talk about this. I can change. I'll do better. Just give me time."

But Emily shook her head, her voice firm but full of sorrow. "I've given you time, Alex. I've given you everything. But I can't keep giving and getting nothing in return."

She turned and walked out the door, leaving Alex standing in the middle of his office, surrounded by everything he had worked so hard to build—and realizing that he had lost the one thing that truly mattered.

In the days that followed, Alex tried to focus on work, to bury his pain in the company, but it was no use. The deal he had been working on fell through, and for the first time, Alex didn't care. The drive, the ambition that had fueled him for so long, was gone, replaced by a deep, aching emptiness. He had spent years climbing the ladder of success, only to find that it had been leaning against the wrong wall.

He tried to reach out to Emily, to apologize, to beg her to come back, but she was done. She loved him, but she couldn't keep sacrificing herself and their daughter for a man who was never really there. Alex was left alone, the silence of his empty home a constant reminder of what he had lost.

It took months for Alex to even begin to pick up the pieces. He stepped back from the company, handed over the reins to his COO, and took a long, hard look at his life. He realized that he had been so focused on winning that he had lost sight of what really mattered. He had let his obsession with success cost him his marriage, his family, and his happiness.

UNSTOPPABLE

But in that painful realization, Alex found a new sense of clarity. He understood that success wasn't about the money, the accolades, or the status. It was about balance, about finding a way to achieve your dreams without losing yourself in the process. It was about being present for the people you love, about making time for what truly matters.

Alex decided to rebuild—not just his life, but himself. He started going to therapy, learning how to let go of the relentless need to prove himself, how to be present in the moment, and how to find peace in simply being, rather than constantly doing. He reached out to old friends, reconnected with his family, and began to mend the relationships he had neglected for so long.

It wasn't easy, and there were days when the regret felt overwhelming. But slowly, Alex began to heal. He found joy in the simple things—spending time with his daughter, cooking dinner at home, taking long walks without the weight of the world on his shoulders. He rediscovered the things that had once made him happy, before success had consumed him.

And in that process, Alex found a new kind of success—a quieter, deeper success that wasn't about winning at all costs, but about living a life that was full and meaningful. He learned that real success isn't measured by what you achieve, but by who you become in the pursuit of those achievements. It's about balance, about knowing when to push and when to pull back, and about understanding that the greatest victories are the ones that happen within.

Alex's story is a reminder that success is a journey, not a destination. It's about finding balance between ambition and contentment, between striving for more and appreciating what you already have. It's about recognizing that the cost of success shouldn't be your happiness, your relationships, or your well-being.

If you're chasing a dream, if you're pushing yourself to the brink in the pursuit of success, take a moment to pause. Look around you. Ask yourself what really matters, and make sure that in your quest to win, you're not losing the things that can't be replaced.

Because the truth is, the greatest success you can achieve is a life well-lived, a life where you're present for the people you love, where you find joy in the journey, and where you never lose sight of what truly matters.

So take a breath, step back, and remember: Success isn't just about reaching the top. It's about enjoying the climb, and making sure that when you get there, the view is worth it.

UNSTOPPABLE

THE QUIET STRUGGLE

FINDING THE STRENGTH TO KEEP GOING WHEN NO ONE BELIEVES IN YOU

We all face moments when it feels like the world is against us—when the people we thought would support us turn away, when our dreams seem too big, too far out of reach. It's in these moments of loneliness and doubt that our true character is forged. This is the story of Rachel, a woman who was on the brink of giving up but found the strength to push through and, in doing so, discovered a path to a success she never imagined.

Rachel wasn't the kind of person who liked to draw attention to herself. She was quiet, thoughtful, and more comfortable in the background than in the spotlight. But she had a dream—a big dream—that she kept tucked away in her heart, afraid to share it with anyone for fear they'd laugh or, worse, tell her it was impossible.

Rachel had always loved to bake. As a child, she spent hours in the kitchen with her grandmother, learning how to make everything from scratch—bread, pies, cookies, you name it. It was her happy place, a refuge from the world where she could lose herself in the rhythm of measuring, mixing, and creating something delicious. But as she grew older, life got in the way. She went to college, got a degree in accounting, and took a steady job at a local firm. Baking became something she did on weekends, a hobby that brought her joy but never seemed like something she could turn into a career.

UNSTOPPABLE

But the dream never left her. It was always there, in the back of her mind, whispering that maybe, just maybe, she could do something more with her life.

One day, after yet another long day at the office, Rachel found herself standing in her tiny kitchen, covered in flour, a tray of freshly baked cookies in front of her. As she tasted one, still warm from the oven, she thought, "What if I could do this every day? What if I could turn this into something real?"

The thought was terrifying, but it was also exhilarating. Rachel knew she was good at baking—everyone who tried her creations said so—but turning that into a business? That was something else entirely. She had no idea where to start, no clue how to turn her passion into a livelihood. But the thought wouldn't go away. It kept nagging at her, pushing her to take a leap of faith.

So, she decided to go for it.

Rachel started small, baking in her free time and selling her treats at local farmers' markets. At first, it was just for fun—a way to test the waters without taking too much risk. But as she started to get more serious about it, she quickly realized that running a business was a lot harder than she had imagined. There were permits to get, licenses to apply for, costs to cover, and on top of that, the constant worry that maybe she was making a huge mistake.

UNSTOPPABLE

But the hardest part wasn't the work. It was the lack of support from the people around her.

When Rachel told her family and friends about her plans, the reactions were mixed, at best. Some were supportive, but most were skeptical. They loved her baking, sure, but a business? That seemed like a stretch.

"Are you sure you want to do this?" her father asked, concern etched on his face. "It's a tough industry. What if it doesn't work out?"

Her friends were no more encouraging. "You've got a good job, Rachel," they said. "Why would you risk that for something so uncertain?"

The doubts were like a weight on her shoulders, pulling her down, making her question everything. She knew they meant well, but every time someone expressed concern, it chipped away at her confidence. Rachel found herself lying awake at night, wondering if they were right. Was she crazy for thinking she could make this work? Was she setting herself up for failure?

UNSTOPPABLE

The turning point came one rainy Saturday morning. Rachel was at the farmers' market, her little stand set up between two much bigger, more established vendors. The rain had kept most people away, and she had only sold a handful of items. She was cold, wet, and tired, and as she looked at the unsold pastries on her table, she felt the doubts creeping in again.

Maybe this was a mistake. Maybe she wasn't cut out for this. Maybe she should just pack up and go home.

But then, something unexpected happened. A woman approached her stand, a small child in tow. The woman looked exhausted, like she hadn't slept in days. She picked up a loaf of Rachel's homemade bread, inhaled deeply, and smiled.

"This smells just like my grandmother's," she said, her voice soft with nostalgia. "I haven't had bread like this in years. Thank you."

The woman's words hit Rachel like a bolt of lightning. In that moment, she realized something important—she wasn't just baking bread. She was creating something that brought people comfort, that reminded them of home, of family, of love. What she was doing mattered, even if it didn't always feel like it. And that was worth fighting for.

UNSTOPPABLE

Rachel decided right then and there that she wasn't going to give up. She was going to keep pushing, keep believing, even when no one else did. She knew it wouldn't be easy, but she also knew that if she gave up now, she'd always wonder what could have been.

The next few months were tough. Rachel worked harder than ever, often late into the night, perfecting her recipes, finding new ways to reach customers, and slowly building a loyal following. It wasn't glamorous, and there were still plenty of setbacks—days when she barely broke even, when the doubts came rushing back, when she wondered if she was fooling herself.

But Rachel kept going, one step at a time. She started getting regular customers, people who came back week after week because they loved what she made. She began catering small events, then bigger ones. Her name started to spread, and soon, she was getting requests from local cafes and restaurants to supply them with her baked goods.

Then came the big break—a local food magazine featured her in an article about up-and-coming artisans. The response was overwhelming. Orders flooded in, and for the first time, Rachel felt like her dream was within reach.

UNSTOPPABLE

With the money she made from the magazine feature, Rachel was able to open her own bakery—a small, cozy shop with a warm, inviting atmosphere. She filled it with the smells of fresh bread and pastries, with the love and care she put into everything she made. The bakery became a gathering place, a community hub where people came not just for the food, but for the feeling of home it gave them.

Rachel's bakery thrived, but more importantly, she found a sense of fulfillment she had never known in her accounting job. She was doing what she loved, on her own terms, and it was making a difference in people's lives. The skeptics who had doubted her, who had questioned her decision to leave a steady job, now came to her shop to buy bread, to congratulate her, to tell her how proud they were of what she had accomplished.

But the real victory wasn't in proving them wrong—it was in proving to herself that she could do it. Rachel had faced her fears, her doubts, and the lack of support from the people around her, and she had come out the other side stronger, wiser, and more determined than ever.

Rachel's story is a reminder that the road to success is often lonely, filled with doubts and setbacks, especially when no one else believes in you. But it's also a reminder that those who persevere, who push through the loneliness and the fear, are the ones who ultimately succeed. It's about finding the strength within yourself to keep going, even when the world seems to be telling you to stop.

UNSTOPPABLE

If you're feeling alone in your journey, if you're facing doubts from those around you, remember Rachel's story. Remember that the most important belief is the one you have in yourself. Keep going, keep pushing, and keep believing that what you're doing matters.

Because the truth is, the world needs more people who are willing to chase their dreams, who are willing to take risks, and who are willing to fight for what they believe in. And if you keep going, if you keep believing, you just might find that the quiet struggle you're going through now is the foundation for the incredible success that's waiting for you.

Your dream is worth the fight. Don't give up. Keep going, and make it happen.

THE ALMOST MILLIONAIRE

WHEN SUCCESS SLIPS THROUGH YOUR FINGERS

There's a certain heartbreak in getting so close to your dreams that you can almost taste them, only to have them slip through your fingers at the last moment. It's the kind of pain that makes you want to give up, to say, "Maybe it wasn't meant to be." But sometimes, it's in those moments of crushing defeat that the seeds of true success are planted. This is the story of Jason, a man who was on the brink of becoming a millionaire, only to lose everything—and then find a way to rebuild that changed his life forever.

Jason had always been a hustler. From a young age, he was the kid who could sell anything to anyone—whether it was lemonade in the summer or snow shoveling services in the winter, he was always looking for a way to make a buck. As he got older, that hustle turned into an entrepreneurial spirit that couldn't be contained. He didn't want a regular 9-to-5; he wanted to build something of his own, something that would make him rich.

By the time he was 30, Jason had started a handful of small businesses—some failed, some did okay, but none of them had taken off the way he had hoped. He was always looking for that one big idea, the one that would finally put him on the map. And then, one day, it came to him.

UNSTOPPABLE

Jason had always been into fitness, and he noticed that there was a growing trend in the health food market. People were becoming more conscious of what they were eating, looking for snacks that were not only tasty but also healthy. That's when he came up with the idea for a protein bar that wasn't just another bland, chalky snack—it would be packed with natural ingredients, full of flavor, and good for you.

He called it "FuelUp," and he believed it was going to be huge.

Jason poured everything he had into the business. He spent months perfecting the recipe, sourcing the best ingredients, and working on branding that would stand out on the shelves. He maxed out his credit cards, took out loans, and even borrowed money from friends and family to get the company off the ground. It was a massive risk, but Jason was convinced it was going to pay off.

And for a while, it looked like he was right.

FuelUp launched with a bang. Jason managed to get his bars into a few local stores, and the feedback was incredible. People loved them. Sales started to climb, and before long, he was in talks with a major grocery chain to distribute FuelUp nationwide. It was the break he had been waiting for—the chance to go from small-time entrepreneur to millionaire practically overnight.

UNSTOPPABLE

The grocery chain loved the product, and after weeks of negotiations, they offered Jason a deal that could change his life. They wanted to place FuelUp in all of their stores across the country, with the potential to expand internationally. The contract was worth millions, and Jason could already see the future he had dreamed of coming to life—fancy cars, a big house, financial freedom.

But there was a catch. The grocery chain needed the first shipment in just six weeks. It was an insanely tight deadline, and Jason knew it would be nearly impossible to meet. But he didn't care—he couldn't pass up this opportunity. He agreed to the terms and threw everything he had into making it happen.

The next six weeks were a blur of chaos. Jason worked around the clock, coordinating production, handling logistics, and managing a growing team. The stress was intense, but he kept pushing, driven by the vision of success that was so close he could almost touch it.

But then, disaster struck.

Two weeks before the shipment was due, there was a problem at the production facility. A key ingredient was delayed, and without it, they couldn't make the bars. Jason scrambled to find a solution, but the clock was ticking, and every hour that passed brought him closer to the deadline with no product to deliver.

He called the grocery chain, explained the situation, and begged for more time. But they were firm—they needed the product on time or the deal was off. Jason tried everything he could to make it work, but in the end, it was no use. The shipment didn't happen, and the grocery chain pulled out of the deal.

Just like that, everything Jason had worked for was gone.

The fallout was devastating. Jason had invested everything into FuelUp, and now, he was left with nothing but debt and a warehouse full of unsold product. He had to lay off his entire team, close the business, and face the reality that his dream of becoming a millionaire had slipped through his fingers.

For weeks, Jason couldn't bring himself to do anything. He felt like a failure, like he had let everyone down—his family, his friends, his investors, and most of all, himself. He couldn't stop replaying the events in his mind, wondering where he had gone wrong, how he had let success slip away when it was right in front of him.

But then, something changed.

UNSTOPPABLE

As he sat in his empty warehouse, surrounded by boxes of unsold protein bars, Jason realized that he had two choices. He could let this failure define him, or he could learn from it and try again. He thought about everything he had accomplished, how close he had come, and he realized that despite the failure, he had learned more from this experience than from anything else in his life.

Jason decided to take what he had learned and start over—but this time, he would do things differently. He reached out to the same grocery chain, not with an apology, but with a new idea. He pitched a smaller, more focused version of FuelUp—starting with just a few stores, with a commitment to grow gradually, ensuring that production could meet demand every step of the way.

To his surprise, they agreed.

With a new, leaner business model and a renewed focus on quality over quantity, Jason relaunched FuelUp. This time, he didn't rush. He took the time to build a strong foundation, learning from the mistakes that had cost him so much the first time around. He focused on creating a product that people truly loved, not just on chasing the next big deal.

And it worked. Slowly but surely, FuelUp began to grow again—this time, sustainably. Sales started to climb, and the grocery chain expanded the product to more stores. Jason didn't become an overnight millionaire, but the business was profitable, and it was growing at a pace he could manage.

UNSTOPPABLE

Within a few years, FuelUp was a well-known brand, and Jason had finally achieved the success he had been chasing for so long. But more importantly, he had done it in a way that allowed him to enjoy the journey, to appreciate the process, and to build something that wasn't just a flash in the pan, but a lasting success.

Jason's story is a powerful reminder that success isn't just about reaching the top—it's about how you handle the setbacks along the way. It's about resilience, about learning from failure, and about having the courage to keep going even when everything seems lost. It's about understanding that sometimes, the path to success is full of twists and turns, and that the real victory comes not from avoiding failure, but from rising above it.

If you're in a place where it feels like your dreams are slipping away, where the setbacks are piling up and the future seems uncertain, remember Jason's story. Remember that even when success seems just out of reach, it's not the end of the road. It's just a detour, an opportunity to regroup, learn, and come back stronger.

Don't give up. Don't let failure define you. Use it as fuel to keep pushing forward, to keep striving for the success that you know is possible.

UNSTOPPABLE

Because the truth is, the only difference between those who succeed and those who don't is the willingness to keep going, to keep believing, and to keep fighting for what you want—even when the odds are against you.

Your success story is still being written. And the best part? The ending is up to you.

30

THE UNSEEN SACRIFICE

WHEN DOING THE RIGHT THING FEELS LIKE THE WRONG MOVE

Sometimes, the hardest decisions are the ones that go unnoticed. The moments when you choose integrity over profit, honesty over success, and doing what's right over what's easy. It's in these quiet, often painful choices that true character is revealed, and the seeds of long-term success are planted, even when it feels like you're losing in the short term. This is the story of Jessica, a woman who made a decision that cost her everything—only to realize it was the best thing she ever did.

Jessica had always been a straight shooter. Growing up in a small town, her parents had instilled in her the values of honesty, hard work, and doing the right thing, no matter the cost. She carried those values with her when she moved to the city, determined to make a name for herself in the competitive world of real estate.

Jessica wasn't just good at her job—she was great. She had a knack for seeing potential where others saw problems, turning rundown properties into profitable investments. Her reputation grew quickly, and within a few years, she had built a solid business with a loyal client base. People trusted Jessica because she was honest, reliable, and always had their best interests at heart.

But then, she was offered a deal that tested everything she believed in.

UNSTOPPABLE

A wealthy developer approached her with a proposition. He had his eye on a piece of land in a rapidly gentrifying neighborhood, a property that Jessica had been managing for an elderly couple who had lived there for over 40 years. The developer wanted to buy the property, tear down the old house, and build luxury condos in its place. The offer was more money than Jessica had ever seen—enough to take her business to the next level, to secure her future, and to finally reach the level of success she had always dreamed of.

But there was a catch.

The couple who owned the property had no intention of selling. The house had been their home for decades, filled with memories, and they couldn't imagine living anywhere else. They trusted Jessica to take care of their home, to look out for their best interests, and she knew that convincing them to sell would be a betrayal of that trust.

Jessica was torn. The money was tempting, and the developer made it clear that if she didn't convince the couple to sell, he'd find another agent who would—and she'd lose the deal. She tried to justify it to herself, telling herself that the couple would be better off with the money, that the neighborhood was changing anyway, that someone else would sell the property if she didn't.

UNSTOPPABLE

But deep down, she knew the truth. Selling the property wasn't the right thing to do—not for the couple, and not for herself. It went against everything she believed in, everything she had built her business on. But walking away from the deal meant walking away from a life-changing opportunity.

After days of agonizing over the decision, Jessica made the call. She met with the developer, thanked him for the offer, and told him she couldn't do it. She couldn't betray the trust of her clients, even if it meant losing the deal. The developer wasn't pleased—he stormed out of the meeting, telling her she was making a huge mistake and that she'd regret it.

And for a while, she did.

The deal fell through, and with it, Jessica's hopes of taking her business to the next level. She lost the client to another agent, and the couple eventually found out about the offer, deciding to sell the property after all—but not with her. The money she had walked away from haunted her, and the frustration of losing the deal made her question if she had done the right thing. She felt like a failure, like she had let herself down, and the business she had worked so hard to build began to struggle.

But then, something unexpected happened.

UNSTOPPABLE

Word started to spread about what Jessica had done. People in the industry, clients, and even the media heard about the agent who had walked away from a lucrative deal because it wasn't the right thing to do. At first, it was just whispers, but soon, it became something more. Jessica began to receive calls from potential clients, not just from her city, but from all over the state—people who wanted to work with someone they could trust, someone who put integrity above profit.

Jessica's business began to grow, slowly at first, but then with a momentum that surprised even her. She started getting referrals from people she didn't even know, clients who valued her honesty and were willing to pay a premium for it. The deals she started to close weren't just big—they were the kind of deals that made a real difference in the community, restoring historic homes, revitalizing neighborhoods, and creating spaces where people wanted to live.

Within a few years, Jessica's business was thriving like never before. She had become one of the most respected agents in the city, known not just for her success, but for the way she achieved it. The same developer who had stormed out on her came back, offering her another deal—this time, on her terms. And the elderly couple, who had moved away, sent her a letter thanking her for her honesty and integrity, telling her that they had finally found peace with their decision because they knew she had done right by them.

UNSTOPPABLE

Jessica had become everything she had ever wanted to be—successful, respected, and proud of the work she was doing. But more importantly, she had built a business that reflected who she was, a business that was rooted in the values her parents had taught her. She hadn't taken the easy road, but she had taken the right one, and in the end, it had led her to a place she couldn't have imagined.

Jessica's story is a powerful reminder that true success isn't just about the money, the deals, or the titles—it's about who you become along the way. It's about making decisions that align with your values, even when it's hard, and trusting that doing the right thing will lead you to the right place, even if it takes time.

If you're facing a decision that feels like a choice between your values and your success, remember Jessica's story. Remember that the hardest decisions are often the most important, and that sometimes, walking away from what seems like a sure thing is the best thing you can do. It might not pay off right away, and it might even feel like a loss in the moment, but in the long run, staying true to yourself is the only way to build a life and a career you can be proud of.

Because the truth is, success built on a foundation of integrity is the only kind of success that lasts. It's the kind of success that brings not just wealth, but fulfillment, not just respect, but peace of mind.

So when you're faced with a choice, when the easy road tempts you, and the pressure to compromise feels overwhelming, take a step back. Remember what matters most, and make the decision that aligns with who you are and who you want to be.

Your future self will thank you for it. And when you look back, you'll see that the sacrifices you made were the building blocks of a life and a legacy that truly matter.

31  THE LATE BLOOMER

FINDING SUCCESS WHEN EVERYONE ELSE HAS MOVED ON

There's a certain kind of pain that comes from watching everyone around you succeed while you're still trying to find your way. It's the feeling that you've missed the boat, that your best years are behind you, and that maybe it's too late to chase your dreams. But sometimes, it's the ones who take the longest to bloom who end up achieving the most. This is the story of David, a man who spent years feeling like he was falling behind, only to discover that his time was coming—just not in the way he expected.

David had always been a dreamer, but he wasn't the kind of person who found success early in life. While his friends were getting promotions, buying houses, and starting families, David was still trying to figure out what he wanted to do with his life. He bounced from job to job, never quite finding the right fit, always feeling like he was on the outside looking in. He had big ideas, sure, but they never seemed to go anywhere, and as the years went by, he started to wonder if he was destined to be one of those people who just never quite made it.

By the time he hit his late 30s, David was working a dead-end job in a call center, answering phones for a company he didn't care about, living paycheck to paycheck in a small apartment. He watched as his friends climbed the corporate ladder, posted pictures of their new homes on social media, and talked about their kids' soccer games, while he was still struggling to pay his rent. He

UNSTOPPABLE

felt like a failure, like he had wasted his potential, and that maybe it was too late to turn things around.

But then, something happened that changed everything.

David had always loved to write. It was the one thing that made him feel alive, the one thing that allowed him to express himself in a way that nothing else could. He had written short stories and poems as a teenager, but as life got busier and responsibilities piled up, he had pushed that passion aside, telling himself he didn't have time for it anymore. But deep down, the desire to write had never gone away—it had just been buried under years of self-doubt and fear.

One night, after a particularly rough day at work, David found himself sitting at his old desk, staring at a blank document on his computer. He didn't know why, but something compelled him to start writing. At first, the words came slowly, awkwardly, like trying to start an engine that hadn't been used in years. But as he kept going, something inside him clicked, and the words started to flow.

He wrote for hours, pouring out all the frustration, the sadness, and the longing he had been carrying for so long. It wasn't perfect—it was messy, raw, and full of emotion—but it felt real. When he finally stopped, the sun was starting to rise, and for the first time in a long time, David felt a sense of peace.

UNSTOPPABLE

Over the next few weeks, David kept writing, each night returning to his computer, letting the words pour out of him. He didn't have a plan, didn't know where it was going, but he didn't care. He was writing for himself, not for anyone else, and that was enough.

Then, one day, he stumbled across an online writing contest. The theme was "second chances," and something about it spoke to him. Without thinking too much about it, he submitted one of his stories—a deeply personal piece about a man who gets a second chance at life after losing everything.

He didn't expect to win. In fact, he almost forgot about it after hitting submit. But a few weeks later, he got an email that made his heart stop. His story had been selected as the winner.

The prize wasn't much—just a small cash award and publication in an online literary magazine—but for David, it felt like a turning point. For the first time, someone outside of himself had recognized his talent, and that validation was like fuel to a fire that had been smoldering for years.

Encouraged by the win, David started submitting his work to other contests and publications. He faced a lot of rejection, but every now and then, a piece would get accepted, and slowly, his confidence began to grow. He started to believe that maybe, just maybe, it wasn't too late for him.

UNSTOPPABLE

As he continued to write, David's work began to attract attention. An editor at a small publishing house reached out to him, asking if he had ever considered writing a novel. The idea terrified him—he had never written anything longer than a short story—but the editor's interest gave him the push he needed to try.

It took him over a year, but David finally finished his first novel—a gritty, heartfelt story about a man's journey to redemption. The editor loved it and offered him a book deal. When the novel was published, it received rave reviews, and for the first time in his life, David felt like he was exactly where he was supposed to be.

The book didn't make him an overnight millionaire, but it did something even more important—it opened the door to a career he had never thought possible. David was finally doing what he loved, and people were paying him for it. He wasn't just writing in the margins of his life anymore—he was living his dream.

As his writing career took off, David began to see his past struggles in a new light. All those years of feeling lost, of not knowing what he wanted to do, had given him the depth and experience to write the stories he was now telling. He realized that his late start wasn't a disadvantage—it was what made his work unique, what gave it the heart and soul that resonated with readers.

UNSTOPPABLE

By the time David hit his 40s, he was doing better than he ever had before. He wasn't just surviving—he was thriving. His books were selling, his bank account was growing, and for the first time in his life, he felt like he was truly successful. But more than that, he had found his purpose, his calling, and that was worth more than any amount of money.

David's story is a reminder that success doesn't have a deadline. It's easy to look at others and feel like you're falling behind, like you've missed your chance, but the truth is, everyone's journey is different. Sometimes, the people who take the longest to find their way are the ones who end up going the farthest.

If you're feeling like time is running out, like you're too old to chase your dreams, remember David's story. Remember that it's never too late to start, and that the experiences you've had along the way are what make you uniquely qualified to succeed. Your story isn't over just because it didn't happen on the timeline you expected.

So keep going. Keep dreaming. Keep believing that your time is coming, because it is. And when it does, you'll look back and realize that every step, every struggle, every moment of doubt was leading you to the place you were always meant to be.

Your journey might not look like everyone else's, but that's what makes it yours. And in the end, that's what will make it worth it.

32 — THE FINAL PUSH

WHEN EVERYTHING HANGS BY A THREAD

There's a point in every journey where it feels like you're hanging by a thread, where every ounce of effort seems futile, and you're left wondering if it's all worth it. It's that moment when the weight of everything you've been through threatens to crush you, and you're forced to make a choice: push through the pain or let go. This is the story of Sarah, a woman who faced the darkest hour of her life, only to find that the breakthrough she desperately needed was just on the other side of her fear.

Sarah had always been a hard worker. Growing up in a blue-collar family, she learned the value of a dollar early on. Her parents had sacrificed everything to give her a better life, and she was determined to make them proud. She was the first in her family to go to college, graduating with a degree in business and dreams of building something big—something that would not only change her life but honor the sacrifices her parents had made.

After college, Sarah moved to the city with nothing but a suitcase and a heart full of ambition. She started out working for a small marketing firm, learning the ropes and saving every penny she could. But deep down, she knew she wasn't meant to work for someone else forever. She had bigger dreams, and after a few years, she finally felt ready to take the leap.

UNSTOPPABLE

With her savings and a small loan, Sarah launched her own marketing agency, focusing on helping small businesses grow. She had a clear vision, a strong work ethic, and a burning desire to succeed. At first, things went well—she landed a few clients, built a small team, and started making a name for herself. But as the months went by, the pressure began to mount.

The competition in the city was fierce, and the bills were piling up faster than the revenue. Sarah found herself working around the clock, taking on more clients than she could handle, and sacrificing her health and personal life just to keep the business afloat. The stress was overwhelming, but she couldn't afford to slow down. She was all in, and failure wasn't an option.

But despite her best efforts, things started to unravel.

One by one, her biggest clients began to drop off, either because they couldn't afford her services anymore or because they found cheaper alternatives. The revenue dried up, and soon, Sarah was struggling just to make payroll. She maxed out her credit cards, took out another loan, and borrowed money from friends and family, all in a desperate attempt to keep the business alive. But no matter what she did, it never seemed to be enough.

Then came the day that brought her to her knees.

UNSTOPPABLE

It was a cold winter morning, and Sarah was sitting in her tiny office, staring at a stack of unpaid bills and a nearly empty bank account. She had just gotten off the phone with yet another client who had decided to go in a different direction, and she knew she was out of options. The loan payments were due, her employees needed to be paid, and she had no idea where the money was going to come from.

For the first time since she started the business, Sarah felt like giving up. The weight of the world was crushing her, and she couldn't see a way out. She had given everything she had—her time, her energy, her money—and it had all come crashing down around her. The dream she had worked so hard to build was slipping through her fingers, and she felt powerless to stop it.

That night, Sarah lay awake in bed, staring at the ceiling, her mind racing with fear and doubt. She thought about all the sacrifices she had made, all the late nights and early mornings, all the times she had pushed through exhaustion and kept going because she believed in her dream. And now, it was all falling apart.

But as she lay there in the darkness, something inside her shifted. She realized that she had two choices: she could let this defeat her, or she could fight back with everything she had. She knew it wasn't going to be easy, and there was no guarantee of success, but she also knew that if she gave up now, she would regret it for the rest of her life.

UNSTOPPABLE

The next morning, Sarah made a decision. She was going to give it one final push—one last, all-out effort to turn things around. If it didn't work, at least she would know she had given it everything she had. But if it did… well, she wasn't ready to give up on that possibility just yet.

Sarah started by reaching out to every contact she had, letting them know about her situation and asking for help. She swallowed her pride and called former clients, offering them discounts and incentives to come back. She spent hours on the phone with potential investors, pitching her business and her vision with a newfound sense of urgency. She even took on a side job, working nights to bring in some extra cash to keep the lights on.

For weeks, Sarah lived on the edge, never knowing if she was going to make it to the next day. But slowly, things began to change. One of her old clients agreed to come back, then another, and then a new client signed on. The investor she had been courting for months finally agreed to meet with her, and after hearing her pitch, he decided to invest.

The money started to trickle in, and with it, a glimmer of hope. Sarah used the funds to pay off her most pressing debts, to keep her team together, and to start rebuilding the business. It was still a struggle, but she could see the tide turning, and that gave her the strength to keep going.

UNSTOPPABLE

Over the next few months, Sarah's business slowly began to recover. The clients kept coming, the revenue started to grow, and the stress that had once consumed her began to lift. She wasn't out of the woods yet, but she was on her way, and for the first time in a long time, she felt like she could breathe again.

And then, something incredible happened.

One of the investors she had pitched to—someone who had initially turned her down—reached out with an offer. He had been watching her progress, impressed by her tenacity and determination, and he wanted to help her take the business to the next level. He offered a significant investment, enough to pay off her debts and give her the capital she needed to expand.

Sarah couldn't believe it. After everything she had been through, after all the nights she had spent wondering if she was going to lose everything, she was finally seeing the light at the end of the tunnel. The investment was a game-changer, and with it, Sarah was able to not only save her business but grow it into something bigger and better than she had ever imagined.

Within a year, Sarah's agency was thriving. She had expanded her team, moved into a bigger office, and was working with clients she had once only dreamed of. The business that had been on the brink of collapse was now one of the most respected agencies in the city, and Sarah was finally living the life she had always wanted.

UNSTOPPABLE

But more than the success, Sarah had found something even more valuable: a deep, unshakeable belief in herself. She had faced the darkest hour of her life, and she had come out the other side stronger, wiser, and more determined than ever. She knew now that she could handle whatever life threw at her, and that knowledge was worth more than any amount of money.

Sarah's story is a testament to the power of perseverance, to the idea that sometimes, the only thing standing between you and success is your willingness to keep going when everything else tells you to stop. It's about understanding that the breakthrough you're looking for might be just on the other side of your fear, and that if you can find the strength to push through, you'll discover that you're capable of more than you ever imagined.

If you're facing your own final push, if you're hanging by a thread and wondering if it's all worth it, remember Sarah's story. Remember that sometimes, the darkest moments are the ones that lead to the greatest triumphs, and that the only way to fail is to give up.

So keep going. Keep fighting. Keep believing that your breakthrough is just around the corner, because it is.

And when you finally get there, when you look back at everything you've been through, you'll realize that every struggle, every setback, and every sleepless night was worth it.

Because in the end, it's not just about the success—it's about the journey, and the strength you find along the way.

33 — THE ALMOST LOSS

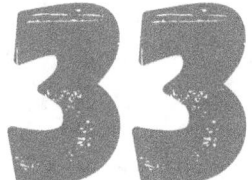

WHEN EVERYTHING YOU BUILT IS ABOUT TO SLIP AWAY

Success can be fragile. Just when you think you've made it, when you're finally standing on solid ground, life can throw you a curveball that threatens to take it all away. It's in these moments of near-loss, when everything you've worked for is on the line, that you discover what you're truly made of. This is the story of Mike, a man who came within inches of losing everything he'd built, only to realize that sometimes, the brink of disaster is where real success is born.

Mike was a self-made man. He didn't come from money or connections—everything he had, he earned through grit and determination. Growing up in a rough neighborhood, he learned early on that if he wanted a better life, he'd have to fight for it. And fight he did. After years of working dead-end jobs, saving every penny, and refusing to let his circumstances define him, Mike finally got his break.

He started a small construction company with just a few employees, taking on whatever jobs he could get. The work was hard, the hours were long, but Mike loved every minute of it. He was building something—not just homes, but a future. And slowly, his reputation grew. Clients appreciated his honesty, his attention to detail, and the way he treated every project like it was his own. Word spread, and before long, Mike's company was one of the most sought-after in the area.

UNSTOPPABLE

For a while, it felt like everything was falling into place. The business was booming, the money was coming in, and Mike was finally able to provide the life for his family that he had always dreamed of. He bought a house in a nice neighborhood, sent his kids to good schools, and even started thinking about expanding the business. But just when it seemed like nothing could go wrong, everything did.

It started with a single project—a large, complex build that was supposed to be the crown jewel of Mike's company. It was a dream job, one that would put his business on the map and secure his future. Mike poured everything into it, sparing no expense to make sure it was perfect. He hired more workers, invested in top-of-the-line materials, and even took out a loan to cover the upfront costs, confident that the payoff would be worth it.

But as the project progressed, things began to unravel. The timeline slipped, unexpected problems cropped up, and the costs started to spiral out of control. The client, who had been easygoing at first, became increasingly demanding, pushing for changes and threatening to pull out if things weren't done exactly to his specifications. Mike found himself working around the clock, trying to keep the project on track, but no matter what he did, it wasn't enough.

Then came the day that shook Mike to his core.

UNSTOPPABLE

The client, frustrated by the delays and cost overruns, sent Mike a letter terminating the contract. Not only was he pulling out of the deal, but he was also refusing to pay for the work that had already been done, claiming that Mike's company had breached the agreement. To make matters worse, he was threatening to sue if Mike didn't refund the money he had already paid.

The news hit Mike like a freight train. He had invested everything into this project—his time, his money, his reputation. If he couldn't get the client to pay, he'd be ruined. The loan payments were coming due, the workers needed to be paid, and there was no way he could cover the costs without the money from the job. The business he had spent years building was on the brink of collapse, and he didn't know how to stop it.

For days, Mike was paralyzed by fear and frustration. He couldn't eat, couldn't sleep, couldn't think of anything except the looming disaster. He had worked so hard, sacrificed so much, and now it was all slipping away. The thought of losing everything was unbearable, and he didn't know if he had the strength to keep fighting.

But then, something changed.

UNSTOPPABLE

One evening, as Mike was sitting alone in his office, surrounded by stacks of unpaid bills and legal threats, he thought about why he had started the business in the first place. It wasn't just about the money or the success—it was about proving to himself and to everyone who had ever doubted him that he could make something of his life. He realized that he wasn't just fighting to save his business—he was fighting to save the life he had built, the future he had promised to his family.

With renewed determination, Mike decided to take control of the situation. He reached out to the client, not with anger or desperation, but with a clear, professional proposal. He laid out the work that had been done, the value it had created, and the reasons for the delays. He offered to meet with the client in person to discuss a fair resolution, knowing that it was his best chance to salvage the deal.

To his surprise, the client agreed to the meeting.

The negotiations were tough, but Mike stayed calm and focused. He listened to the client's concerns, acknowledged the mistakes that had been made, and worked out a compromise that allowed both sides to walk away satisfied. The client agreed to pay a portion of the outstanding balance, enough to cover Mike's costs and keep the business afloat.

It wasn't the outcome Mike had hoped for, but it was enough to keep him in the game.

UNSTOPPABLE

With the immediate crisis averted, Mike turned his attention to rebuilding the business. He learned from the experience, tightening up his contracts, managing his projects more carefully, and being more selective about the jobs he took on. He also worked hard to rebuild his reputation, reaching out to old clients, offering discounts, and proving that he was still the same trustworthy, hardworking guy they had always known.

Slowly, things started to turn around. The jobs came back, the money started to flow, and the business that had been on the brink of collapse began to thrive once again. But this time, Mike was different. He had faced his worst fears, and he had come out the other side stronger, smarter, and more resilient.

A year later, Mike's company was busier than ever, and he had finally paid off the debt from the disastrous project. The business was solid, his reputation restored, and his confidence renewed. He knew now that he could handle anything that came his way, and that knowledge was worth more than any contract or payday.

Mike's story is a powerful reminder that success isn't just about the victories—it's about how you handle the setbacks. It's about understanding that sometimes, the brink of disaster is where you find your true strength, and that the moments when you think you're about to lose everything are the moments when you discover what you're really capable of.

UNSTOPPABLE

If you're facing a situation where everything feels like it's slipping away, where the pressure is overwhelming and the future uncertain, remember Mike's story. Remember that you have the power to turn things around, to find a way forward even when it feels like all is lost.

Don't give up. Don't let fear and frustration control you. Take a deep breath, assess the situation, and make a plan. You've come this far, and you have the strength to keep going.

Because the truth is, the greatest successes often come on the heels of the greatest challenges. And when you look back, you'll realize that the moments when you almost lost it all were the moments that made you who you are.

Your breakthrough is just a decision away. Keep pushing, keep believing, and keep fighting for the life you've built.

Because it's worth it.

34

THE BOTTOM OF THE BARREL

WHEN ROCK BOTTOM BECOMES YOUR LAUNCHPAD

Rock bottom isn't just a place of despair; it's where the old you dies and the new you is born. It's the point where you either give up or find a way to rise, using the rubble of your past as the foundation for something extraordinary. This is the story of Lisa, a woman who found herself at the lowest point in her life, only to realize that it was the perfect place to start building the life she had always dreamed of.

Lisa wasn't supposed to end up here. She was the overachiever, the one who had always done everything right. She graduated at the top of her class, got a prestigious job at a top-tier law firm, and was on the fast track to becoming a partner by the time she was 30. Her future was bright, her path clear, and everything was going according to plan—until it wasn't.

It started with small cracks in the facade. The long hours at the firm, the constant pressure to bill more hours, to win more cases, and to climb higher and higher on the corporate ladder began to take a toll. Lisa was always exhausted, always stressed, and the passion she once had for her work began to fade. But she kept pushing, kept telling herself that it would all be worth it in the end.

Then, out of nowhere, her life started to unravel.

UNSTOPPABLE

The first blow came when her father, the man who had been her biggest supporter, was diagnosed with a terminal illness. Lisa tried to balance work with caring for him, but the strain was too much. She began to miss deadlines, her performance slipped, and her once-stellar reputation at the firm began to tarnish. Her bosses were sympathetic at first, but as the months went by, their patience wore thin.

The second blow came when her relationship of five years fell apart. Her partner, tired of always being second to her career, decided he couldn't do it anymore. The breakup was messy and left Lisa feeling more alone than she had ever felt in her life. She had sacrificed so much for her career, and now it seemed like she was losing everything that mattered to her.

But the final blow, the one that brought her to her knees, came when she was called into a meeting with the partners. They were letting her go. The firm had decided that Lisa was no longer the rising star she once was and that they couldn't afford to keep her on. Just like that, her career—her entire identity—was stripped away.

Lisa left the office that day with nothing but a box of her belongings and a hollow feeling in her chest. She had hit rock bottom. Her father was dying, her relationship was over, and the career she had spent years building was gone. She didn't know what to do, where to go, or how to start over.

UNSTOPPABLE

For weeks, Lisa stayed in her small apartment, barely leaving, barely eating, and barely functioning. She felt like a failure, like everything she had worked for had been for nothing. She was scared, lost, and completely broken.

But then, something happened that she never expected.

One evening, while mindlessly scrolling through social media, Lisa came across an article about a woman who had started a successful online business after losing her job. The woman had turned her passion into a thriving company, and her story struck a chord with Lisa. She realized that she had a choice—she could let this be the end of her story, or she could use it as the beginning of something new.

Lisa decided to do something she had never allowed herself to do before: she listened to her heart. For years, she had suppressed her love for art, telling herself that it wasn't practical, that it wasn't something she could ever make a living from. But now, with nothing left to lose, she decided to take a chance.

She dusted off the old sketchbooks she had tucked away in the back of her closet, set up a small studio in her apartment, and started painting again. At first, it was just a way to pass the time, to distract herself from the pain of everything she had lost. But the more she painted, the more she realized how much she loved it, how much it had always been a part of who she was.

UNSTOPPABLE

Lisa began to post her work online, sharing it with friends and family. To her surprise, people loved it. She started getting requests for commissions, small at first, but then more and more as word spread. Encouraged by the positive response, she decided to take it a step further.

She launched an online store, selling prints of her artwork, and to her astonishment, the orders started pouring in. People connected with her work in a way she never imagined, and what had started as a way to cope with her pain was turning into something real, something that could actually support her.

As the months went by, Lisa's business grew. She began collaborating with other artists, selling her work in galleries, and even licensing her designs to companies. She wasn't just surviving —she was thriving. The career she had thought she wanted was gone, but in its place, she had built something that was more fulfilling, more meaningful, and more aligned with who she really was.

And the best part? She was finally happy. For the first time in years, Lisa felt like she was living a life that was true to herself, one that wasn't dictated by the expectations of others or the relentless pursuit of success. She had found her passion, and she had turned it into a life she loved.

UNSTOPPABLE

Lisa's story is a reminder that rock bottom isn't the end—it's the place where you have the opportunity to rebuild, to start over, and to create something better than what you had before. It's about understanding that sometimes, losing everything is the best thing that can happen to you, because it forces you to find out what really matters.

If you're in a place where it feels like everything is falling apart, where you don't know how to move forward, remember Lisa's story. Remember that the lowest points in your life can be the launchpad for your greatest successes, and that sometimes, the only way to find your true path is to let go of the one you thought you were supposed to be on.

Don't be afraid to start over. Don't be afraid to follow your heart, even if it means taking a risk, even if it means stepping into the unknown. Because the truth is, you have the power to turn your pain into something beautiful, to take the rubble of your past and use it to build a future that's better than anything you could have imagined.

Your rock bottom can be your turning point. Keep going, keep believing, and keep creating the life you've always wanted.

Because the best stories are the ones that rise from the ashes.

UNSTOPPABLE

35 — THE LAST CHANCE

WHEN YOU'RE DOWN TO YOUR FINAL BET

There's a certain desperation that sets in when you're down to your last chance—when you've tried everything, fought every battle, and it still feels like the odds are stacked against you. It's the moment when you have to decide whether to fold and walk away or to go all in, risking everything for that one final shot at your dreams. This is the story of Jake, a man who found himself with nothing left to lose, and in that moment of desperation, discovered the courage to make the biggest bet of his life.

Jake had always been a fighter. He wasn't the smartest guy in the room, but he was determined, and he had the kind of work ethic that made people take notice. He had grown up in a small town where opportunities were few and far between, but that hadn't stopped him from dreaming big. Jake wanted more out of life, and he was willing to do whatever it took to get it.

After high school, Jake left his hometown with nothing but a duffel bag and a few hundred dollars in his pocket. He bounced around from job to job, trying to find his footing in a world that seemed determined to knock him down. He worked construction, waited tables, and even did a stint as a car salesman, but nothing seemed to stick. He was always scraping by, always one paycheck away from disaster.

UNSTOPPABLE

But Jake never gave up on his dream of making it big. He had an idea—a business idea that had been simmering in his mind for years. It wasn't anything revolutionary, but it was something he believed in, something that could change his life if he could just figure out how to make it work. He wanted to start a mobile auto repair service, a business that would bring mechanics directly to customers' doors, saving them the hassle of going to a shop.

It sounded simple enough, but getting it off the ground was a different story. Jake didn't have the money, the connections, or the experience to make it happen, and every time he tried to get it going, something seemed to go wrong. He maxed out his credit cards, borrowed from friends, and even took out a high-interest loan, but the business never took off the way he had hoped. The clients were few, the bills were piling up, and the pressure was crushing him.

By the time Jake hit his mid-thirties, he was at the end of his rope. The debt collectors were calling, his car was on the verge of being repossessed, and he was two months behind on rent. The business that was supposed to save him had become an albatross around his neck, dragging him down deeper and deeper into a pit of despair. He had poured everything into this dream, and it was slipping away.

UNSTOPPABLE

One rainy afternoon, as Jake sat in his tiny apartment staring at the stack of overdue bills, he felt something inside him break. The fight had gone out of him, and for the first time in his life, he considered giving up. Maybe this was it. Maybe he wasn't meant to succeed. Maybe he should just throw in the towel, declare bankruptcy, and go back to his hometown with his tail between his legs.

But as he sat there, drenched in hopelessness, Jake remembered something his father had told him years ago, when he was just a kid. "Son, the only time you really lose is when you stop trying. As long as you're still in the game, there's always a chance."

Those words echoed in his mind, cutting through the fog of despair. Jake realized that he wasn't ready to give up—not yet. He had come too far, sacrificed too much, and he couldn't walk away without giving it one final shot. If he was going to fail, he was going to go down swinging.

Jake decided to bet everything on one last move—something he had been too scared to try before. He had heard about a startup competition in the city, a pitch contest where entrepreneurs could present their business ideas to a panel of investors. The prize was a $100,000 investment, enough to pay off his debts, relaunch his business, and finally give him the chance to make his dream a reality.

UNSTOPPABLE

The competition was fierce. Hundreds of entrepreneurs, all with big ideas and even bigger dreams, were vying for the same prize. Jake knew the odds were slim, but he also knew that this was his last chance. He spent the next few days refining his pitch, working late into the night, pouring over every detail, every word, determined to make it perfect.

When the day of the competition arrived, Jake walked into the crowded room with his heart pounding in his chest. He felt like an outsider among the polished, confident contestants, most of whom had fancy business degrees and impressive resumes. But he reminded himself that he had something they didn't—he had nothing left to lose.

Jake's turn came, and he took the stage, the bright lights shining down on him, the faces of the investors staring up at him, waiting to be impressed. He took a deep breath, steadied himself, and launched into his pitch. He talked about his business idea, his vision, and the struggles he had faced trying to make it work. But more than that, he talked about why it mattered—why he believed in it, why he wasn't ready to give up, and why he needed this chance to prove himself.

When he finished, there was a long, agonizing silence. The investors whispered among themselves, scribbling notes, their expressions unreadable. Jake stood there, his heart in his throat, waiting for the verdict.

UNSTOPPABLE

Finally, the lead investor spoke. "Jake, I've seen a lot of pitches today, but yours stood out. Not because it's the most polished or the most innovative, but because it's real. You've put everything on the line, and that kind of determination is something we can't ignore. We're willing to take a chance on you."

Jake could hardly believe what he was hearing. The room erupted in applause, but he barely noticed. All he could think about was that he had done it—he had fought his way back from the brink, and now he had a real shot at making his dream come true.

The $100,000 investment changed everything. Jake used the money to pay off his debts, buy new equipment, and rebrand his business. He hired a small team, expanded his services, and started marketing to a wider audience. Within months, the clients started rolling in, and for the first time, Jake's business was profitable. The stress that had weighed him down for so long began to lift, and he finally felt like he was on solid ground.

But more than the money or the success, what mattered most to Jake was the knowledge that he had fought back. He had stared failure in the face, and instead of backing down, he had bet on himself—and won. The experience had changed him, made him stronger, more resilient, and more determined than ever to keep pushing forward.

UNSTOPPABLE

Jake's story is a testament to the power of perseverance, to the idea that sometimes, your final bet is the one that changes everything. It's about understanding that even when it feels like you've hit rock bottom, there's always a way out if you're willing to keep fighting, to keep believing, and to take that one last shot.

If you're facing your own last chance, if you're feeling like you've tried everything and the odds are against you, remember Jake's story. Remember that as long as you're still in the game, there's always a chance. Don't give up. Don't walk away. Make that final bet, and give it everything you've got.

Because sometimes, when you're down to your last chance, that's when you're closest to the breakthrough you've been waiting for.

Your final bet could be the one that changes everything. Keep fighting, keep believing, and take the risk.

Because the best is yet to come.

UNSTOPPABLE

THE TURNING POINT

WHEN THE MOMENT YOU'VE BEEN WAITING FOR FINALLY ARRIVES

There's a moment in every success story when everything changes —a turning point where all the struggles, the setbacks, and the heartbreaks finally pay off. It's the moment when you realize that everything you've been through was leading you to this point, and the life you've dreamed of is finally within reach. This is the story of Emily, a woman who spent years fighting for her dream, only to discover that sometimes, the breakthrough you've been waiting for comes when you least expect it.

Emily had always been a fighter. She grew up in a small town with big dreams, determined to make something of herself despite the odds. She wanted to be a fashion designer, to create beautiful clothes that made people feel confident and powerful. But in a town where everyone followed the same path, Emily's dreams seemed out of reach. People told her she was crazy, that she should settle for something more practical, but she couldn't let go of her vision.

After high school, Emily moved to the city with nothing but a suitcase full of sketches and a heart full of hope. She worked odd jobs to pay the bills while she tried to break into the fashion industry, but the road was tougher than she had imagined. She sent her designs to every fashion house she could think of, only to be met with rejection after rejection. "Your work is good, but we're not looking for new designers right now," they said. It was the same story over and over, and each rejection chipped away at her confidence.

UNSTOPPABLE

But Emily didn't give up. She kept sketching, kept sewing, and kept dreaming. She believed that if she worked hard enough, if she pushed through the pain and frustration, she would eventually catch a break. And then, after years of grinding, she got her chance—or so she thought.

A small boutique in the city agreed to carry her line. It wasn't a big name, but it was something, and Emily poured everything she had into making it a success. She spent months designing, sewing, and promoting her clothes, dreaming of the day when they would sell out and she would finally be on her way. But when the launch day came, it was a disaster. The boutique was nearly empty, and by the end of the day, she had sold only a handful of pieces.

Devastated, Emily walked home that night in the pouring rain, her dreams feeling more distant than ever. She had given everything she had, and it still wasn't enough. She felt like a failure, like all her hard work had been for nothing. But as she lay in bed that night, soaked and exhausted, something inside her refused to let go. She couldn't stop now—not when she had come this far.

A few weeks later, just when Emily was beginning to think about packing it all in, she got an email that changed everything. A well-known fashion influencer had come across her clothes in the boutique and fallen in love with them. She wanted to feature Emily's line on her social media channels, and she was offering to do it for free because she believed in Emily's vision.

UNSTOPPABLE

Emily could hardly believe it. She had been following this influencer for years, admiring her work and dreaming of the day when she might get a shoutout. And now, that day had arrived.

The next week, the influencer posted a series of photos and videos wearing Emily's designs, tagging her and raving about the quality and style of the clothes. The response was immediate and overwhelming. Emily's phone started buzzing with notifications—likes, comments, messages, and, most importantly, orders. Her website, which had been all but deserted, was suddenly flooded with traffic, and within days, her entire collection was sold out.

For the first time in her life, Emily felt like she had made it. The orders kept coming, and she quickly realized that she needed help to keep up with the demand. She hired a small team, moved into a larger studio, and began expanding her line. The momentum kept building, and before long, Emily's designs were being worn by celebrities, featured in magazines, and sold in boutiques across the country.

But the real turning point wasn't just the success—it was the realization that all the struggles, the heartbreaks, and the near-misses had been leading her to this moment. If she had given up when things got tough, if she had let the rejections and failures define her, she would never have reached this point. It was the fight, the persistence, and the refusal to give up that had brought her here.

UNSTOPPABLE

Emily's story is a reminder that success doesn't come easy, and it doesn't come fast. It's about the grind, the setbacks, and the moments when you think you can't go on—but you do, because there's something inside you that refuses to quit. It's about understanding that the turning point often comes when you least expect it, and that the breakthrough you've been waiting for is closer than you think.

If you're feeling like you've been pushing and fighting for so long with nothing to show for it, remember Emily's story. Remember that every step you take, every battle you fight, is bringing you closer to the moment when everything changes. It's not about how fast you get there—it's about the journey, and the strength you find along the way.

Keep going. Keep believing. Keep pushing through the pain and frustration, because your turning point is coming.

And when it does, you'll look back and realize that every struggle, every setback, was worth it.

Because success isn't just about the destination—it's about who you become on the journey. And that's a story worth telling.

So don't stop now. You're closer than you think.

The best is yet to come.

THE JOURNEY CONTINUES

Success isn't a destination; it's a journey—a journey that never truly ends. It's about more than just reaching your goals; it's about what you learn, who you become, and how you grow along the way. The stories you've read are just the beginning. Each one of these individuals faced their own unique challenges, battled their own demons, and discovered that the road to success is often paved with setbacks, heartache, and moments of doubt. But they also found that it's these very struggles that make the victories so much sweeter.

As you close this book, I want you to remember something important: your story is still being written. You may not have reached your turning point yet. You might be in the middle of your darkest hour, questioning whether you have the strength to keep going. Or maybe you're on the brink of a breakthrough, waiting for that one moment that will change everything.

Wherever you are on your journey, know that you have the power to keep moving forward. Every setback is an opportunity to learn, every failure is a stepping stone, and every challenge is a chance to prove to yourself what you're truly capable of. The people in these stories didn't start out as millionaires—they started out just like you, with dreams, doubts, and a determination to keep going no matter what.

UNSTOPPABLE

Life will throw obstacles in your path. It will test you, push you to your limits, and make you question whether your dreams are worth it. But if there's one thing these stories have shown, it's that the biggest successes often come from the biggest challenges. The key is to keep going, to keep believing in yourself, and to never lose sight of the dream that drives you.

Your journey is unique, and so is your story. Whether you're just starting out, struggling to find your way, or standing at the edge of your breakthrough, remember that you are the author of your own life. You have the power to shape your future, to overcome the odds, and to achieve the kind of success that goes beyond just money or status.

Success isn't just about what you achieve—it's about who you become along the way. It's about resilience, perseverance, and the courage to keep going when things get tough. It's about finding joy in the journey, even when the road is rough, and knowing that every step you take is bringing you closer to the life you've always wanted.

So as you close this book, take a moment to reflect on your own journey. Think about where you've been, where you are now, and where you want to go. And remember that no matter how many times you stumble, no matter how many setbacks you face, you have the strength to rise again.

The journey continues. And your best chapter is still ahead.

Keep writing it. Keep living it. And never, ever give up.

Because the best is yet to come.

Believe. Persist. Thrive.

www.ingramcontent.com/pod-product-compliance
Lightning Source LLC
Chambersburg PA
CBHW052151220526
45471CB00004B/1624